BAHA'U'LLAH AND THE BAB CONFRONT MODERN THINKERS

Book II

SPINOZA: CONCERNING GOD

By the Same Author:

The Great Prophets

Zoroaster's Influence on Greek Thought

*Zoroaster's Influence on Anaxagoras, The Greek
Tragedians, and Socrates*

*The Revelation of Baha'h'ulah and the Bab -
Book One: Descartes' Theory of Knowledge*

BAHA'U'LLAH AND THE BAB CONFRONT MODERN THINKERS

Book II

Spinoza: Concerning God

Ruhi Muhsen Afnan

Philosophical Library
New York

Copyright, 1977, by PHILOSOPHICAL LIBRARY, INC.,
15 East 40 Street, New York, N.Y.10016

Library of Congress Catalog Card No. 75-109166

SBN 8022-2197-1

Manufactured in the United States of America

To the Memory of the Master
Abdul Baha Abbas

TABLE OF CONTENTS.

The primary premises of Ethics should be certain and not hypothetical.— 17

CHAPTER II: SPINOZA'S DEFINITIONS: 1. Spinoza claims to start his system with God.—2. Spinoza indirectly asserts with Descartes the paramountcy of reason.—3. To know is to dominate.—4. The Bab starts with the principle that God's essence is unknowable.—5. Spinoza was dominated by the Greek conception of the universe and its causation.—6. The conception of the universe as the "All" in the light of the teachings of the Bab.—7. "Causa sui" applies to the universe as conceived, and deified, by the Greeks, not to the God of revealed religion.—8. "Causa sui" may be identified with the prophets, as founders of revealed religion.—9. Spinoza considers the sensible and the intelligible limited only by realities of their kind.—10. Thought and body acquire reality when combined.—11. Creation is to impose form on matter, or thought on body, to generate a new individual entity.—12. Spinoza's definition of substance and its emanantal nature.—13. The definition of substance according to the doctrine of creation.—14. The nature of substance when considered as object of thought.—15. In the contingent world of creation, motion is criterion of substantiality.—16. Creation is the supreme form of motion.—17. The type of motion of the substance defines its stage of being.—18. Spinoza's definition of attribute is conceptual and static.—19. Spinoza conceived the created as "mode" of the Creator.— 20. The created cannot be considered as a "mode" of the Creator.—21. Spinoza's definition of "mode" would apply to the divine nature revealed in the prophets.—22. Spinoza's definition of God.—23. Ethics demands a supreme reality which is definable.—24. Infinity of God's attributes.—25. The predicament in explaining the existence of "body" is entailed by the doctrine of emanation.—26. A transcendent reality cannot be limited by an inferior one.—27. Time and space are concomitant of creation.—28. The principle of emanation disregards the reality of time.—29. Spinoza's definition of freedom and necessity.—30. Even in religion no freedom is maintained when the principle of emanation operates.—31. Freedom and causality are interrelated, and their field of operation is the world of creation.—32. The field of freedom is the spiritual and cultural life of man.—33. The creator is free in the pursuit of his creative purpose.—34. Freedom is to the extent man participates in creation.—35. The spiritual and cultural life of man is the result of divine guidance not of coertion.—36. Efficient cause is "compelling," formal

FOREWORD.

Plato, as an Idealist and Rationalist, used the analogy of a captain steering his boat to express the absolute and unchanging character of the human soul in guiding its course through constantly changing conditions of life. To Plato, this unchanging character of the soul, in that constantly changing environment, gave it a semblance of divinity. Like an "idea," such as The Good, the soul seemed unchanging and absolute. Such Idealism conceived the human soul as part and particle of the divine substance, retaining its essential reality, through constant change and improvement. This conception of the soul, which gave it a character beyond the realm of contingency, did not satisfy Aristotle. This latter denied that the captain occupies a position beyond the boat. He conceived the captain as an unchanging "idea" or form, but immanent and standing within the boat, and leading it to its ultimate destiny. In other words, Aristotle conceived the human soul as a reality, retaining its substantial identity, even though immanent in the body, and seemingly moving with it.

As we have observed in the first Book of the series on the Revelation of Baha'u'llah and The Bab, Descartes reverted from the prevailing Aristotalian conception to the Platonic one, and maintained the duality of matter and mind with a sort of parallelism prevailing between them. But this principle was a metaphysical one which revealed religion could not countenance and accept. Spinoza's conception of God was an attempt to justify the importance of monism as ground for the ethical life. Through him that basic conception permeated European thought and acquired a lasting significance. For upon that assumption later systems were built up. Even William James, in his *Varieties of Religious Experiences,* tends to identify psychological with spiritual, or religious phenomena and thereby approach the immanental conception of God.

Baha'u'llah, upholding the basic distinction between the creator and the created, refutes this basic principle of immanence, and considers the human soul as a fully contingent reality, subject to change in its course of creation, sustenance, death and rebirth. He considers the contradictory view of philosophy, of identifying mental with the religious phenomena, as an intellectual aberration that has overcome and viciated human thought in the present age. For every individual who feels some inner psychological experience is apt to consider it religious and of spiritual divine origin.

Jesus said, "He that cometh from above is above all: he that is of the earth is earthly, and speaketh of the earth." (John 3:31). He does not make an exception of the human soul and consider it divine in substance. The Bab is clear on the subject when he says that "other than God is creation." Thus, the human soul, with its intellectual function which we term mind, is just as much part of the contingent world of being, subject to creation, sustenance, death and rebirth, as a plant, though each has its specific measure of perfection and nature of development. The spiritual nature of the prophets, however, is from "above," and beyond that contingency. It is a revelation of the primal purpose of God, and done with Him in substance and nature. Speaking in the name of all the prophets Baha'u'llah says in his *Hidden Words*: "O Son of Man! Veiled in My immemorial being and in the ancient eternity of My essence I knew My love for thee; therefore I created thee, have engraved on these Mine image and revealed to thee My beauty."

And as we proceed we shall observe that through the creative conception the predicaments Monism generates are avoided in tracing the ethical life of man, which is the main objective of such discussions.

BAHA'U'LLAH AND THE BAB CONFRONT MODERN THINKERS

BOOK II.

SPINOZA: CONCERNING GOD.

INTRODUCTION.

1. UNITY OF REASON AND REVELATION IN EARLY CHRISTIANITY

St. Paul, St. John, and some early Church Fathers, such as Justin Martyr and Clement of Alexandria, who were nearest to the source of Christian revelation and explained its various doctrines, were not ignorant of ancient or contemporary philosophic thought. Some of the Fathers actually started their intellectual life as professional teachers of philosophy. They embraced the Faith only after personal study and inner conviction. None of these advocated separation between the field of reason and that of revelation. In fact, they all found in the revelation of Jesus Christ the sole means for settling the predicaments which confronted reason and which had been received as intellectual heritage left by ancient Greek thought. One such predicament was how a factually unknown and unknowable God could act as a source of positive values of the spiritual and cultural life of man. While in Athens, then the center of pagan thought, St. Paul pointed to Jesus Christ as a fully knowable revelation of that unknowable God, and hence the mainspring of that life. Another such pagan predicament was to locate the source of illumination, which Plato had expressed in such lyric language: the repository of all innate Ideas, such as the Good, the True, the Just and the Beautiful; and which Aristotle had defined as the Form of all forms. St. John designated Jesus Christ and identified him with "the Word," or source of man's rational life, the "light" or mainspring of illumination, the "truth" or storehouse of innate ideas, and "the path" or means of attaining a knowledge of the Father and understanding His will and purpose. St.

1

John recognized in Jesus Christ the Form of all forms which Aristotle sought, as culmination of his philosophical system. The early Fathers of the Church contacted Christianity when it was still pure and undefiled by human traditions and interpretations. The study of Greek thought, whether Platonic, Aristotelian, or otherwise, had awakened them to these predicaments, which baffled reason; and they found their adequate solution only in Christian revelation, in the words of Jesus who said: "I am the way, the truth, and the life: no man cometh unto the Father, but by me"(1). "All things are delivered unto me of my Father: and no man knoweth the Son, but the Father; neither knoweth any man the Father, save the Son, and he to whomsoever the Son will reveal him"(2). Thus, to all the early Fathers of the Church, who were well-versed in Greek thought, revelation was a source of illumination which reason could not disregard with impunity. Revelation provided the ultimate notions regarding the nature of God and the reality and destiny of man which unaided reason could not discover, and without which this latter could not attain truth and certainty, and formulate its spiritual and cultural values.

2. GREEK THOUGHT WAS THE PRODUCT OF INDEPENDENT HUMAN REASON.

Greek philosophy claims to have come into being in utter disregard of revealed religion which determined its nature and the trend of its various systems of thought. Within the precincts of Western Hellas where it flourished, there was no revealed religion from which reason could derive its spiritual and cultural values, and with which it could conform. Prior to the dawn of Greek thought Zoroastrianism had appeared in the East and its culture was gradually engulfing all the Hellenic states of Asia Minor. But the founders of Greek philosophy were those who either fled before its onrush, or were irresponsive to its spiritual and cultural call. Greek thought was, therefore, in the main, based upon a culture that was essentially pagan, reacting adversely to the rise of a revealed religion, and attempting to formulate its systems independently; rather than one which diligently sought guidance in the revealed Word, as source of its inspiration and primary premises. It was a self-assertion of reason, in utter disregard of revelation and its basic conceptions regarding the nature of God and of the reality and destiny of man. It created independent systems of its own based upon certain hypotheses irrespective of religious beliefs. But such systems led invariably to predicaments it could not overcome and problems it could not solve. In other words, philosophy disregarded revelation, but could not fully satisfy reason in its search for sound spiritual and cultural values. It had pride in its independence, but ended in impasses.

Such also has been the fate of modern European thought after separating the field of reason from that of revelation, after denying reason illumination on ultimate issues, such as the nature of God and the reality and destiny of man, issues in which revelation can claim the right to advance some truths. Modern thought has tabooed the name of the prophets from books on philosophy and slighted their claim to be "light" by understanding, the "way" to an adequate knowledge of the divine attributes which constitute the virtues man has to acquire and the "path" to human salvation and spiritual regeneration. Modern thought has given preference to pagan premises, and as a result fallen headlong into the very predicaments that had confronted pagan philosophy in ancient days, and gradually caused its deterioration and bankruptcy. One such pagan premise of thought was that man is the measure of all things which we found exemplified in the system of Descartes. Another such premise is the doctrine of emanation of the intellectual and physical universe from God as the source of all being, which we shall see reveal its moral consequences in the Ethics of Spinoza, and here undertake to expound.

3. THE DOCTRINE OF EMANATION ESTABLISHES THE ONTOLOGICAL GROUND OF REVELATION

The principle of revelation is derived from that of emanation and God's desire to express His will and purpose to man. The two doctrines, therefore, may be considered as necessarily implying one another. When emanation or outpouring of the divine essence is, as regarded by revealed religion, restricted to the divine nature of the prophets, then revelation is also confined to it, and the prophets are deemed to be the sole sources of the revealed Word of God. If, on the other hand, emanation is considered a universal principle, comprising the human soul as well, as Neoplatonism and mystic schools generally maintain, then revelation extends to all humanity, and individual human intellect may be regarded as the repository of divine wisdom and understanding, and hence, a source of revelation. It is completely otherwise when the doctrine of creation is main-

3

tained. For a created reality does not partake of the divine substance and essence; hence, by no flight of imagination can it be considered as the mouthpiece of God, and the source of His revealed Word.

4. PAGAN THOUGHT FAILED TO DISTINGUISH BETWEEN PROCEEDING FROM GOD THROUGH THE PROCESS OF EMANATION AND PROCEEDING THROUGH CREATION, AND HENCE MADE NO DISTINCTION BETWEEN REVELATION AND HUMAN REASON

Plato considered "the many" as proceeding from "the One" through the process of division or fission, producing microcosms which qualitatively were "the same" as the macrocosm. In other words, the difference between God, as "the One," and the individual human souls as "the many," was only in number and magnitude, not in form and substance. Hence, an idea, or form, which resided in "the One," resided also in "the many;" though in the latter it was in a hidden, latent, and potential state of being. And such being his belief, he could not have attributed any distinction to the divine nature revealed in the prophets. As a consequence, human reason was to him qualitatively identical with revelation of the Word and the source of Wisdom and Understanding. On the contrary, when the human soul is regarded as it is by revealed religion, a creation of God, made and formed by Him, then there can be no qualitative resemblance between the two. The created human soul becomes a mere product, or artifact, of the Creator as source of its being. In short, to eliminate any equivocation of the term revelation, we should ascertain to what basic doctrine, proceeding from God, it refers: whether the principle of emanation is viewed as confined to the divine nature of the prophets; or whether it is extended to comprise natural objects, including the human soul. For the one is a basic doctrine of revealed religion and the other is fully pagan in origin and tendency.

5. THE RISE OF NEOPLATONISM

Roman Emperors, such as Decius and Valarian, who reigned about the middle of the third century after Christ, had tried to save pagan culture by persecuting the Christians. But all their efforts had proved vain. The more they used force and added to the number of martyrs, the more the new Faith obtained momentum, and added to its adherents. When Gallianus came to power in 260 A.D. he put an end to that useless persecution and decided that the growth of a movement such as Christianity can be checked only by raising the conflict to its field of thought and spirituality. The basis of Christian belief was the sanctity attributed to the divine nature revealed in Jesus Christ, in utter distinction from the rest of mankind. That divine nature was considered an emanation, or manifestation, of God and the channel of His revealed Word. Therefore, Gallianus thought, the only way to combat Christianity effectively, and indirectly displace Jesus Christ from his peculiar place of eminence, was to put all members of the human race on the same level, that is, consider every individual human soul as an emanation of God, as a microcosm qualitatively similar to the macrocosm, and proceeding from it through the process of fission or division. Mystic schools of thought, from immemorial days, held such doctrine of universal emanation from the divine substance. Gallianus had been himself initiated into such a mystic school, and was an ardent believer in such a pagan conception. Neoplatonism, besides holding the principle of emanation as a universal process proceeding from God and applicable to the human soul as well, could put a claim to rationalism, which contrasted with the emotionalism Christians seemed to display in their attitude towards mounting persecution. For it considered the supreme Being in the nature of Mind, and its emanations as "Intelligences." These two basic doctrines, namely, universal emanation of all being from God, and rationalism, commended themselves to Gallianus as the supreme points on which Christianity could be fought and overcome. He, therefore, welcomed Plotinus to Rome, patronized him, and sponsored his many activities among the elite in Rome. Plotinus, thus, undertook to lead the spiritual and cultural struggle against the ever-growing influence of Christianity. After him his student Porphyry took up the task, but it was all in vain. Neoplatonism had no spiritual and cultural values to match Christianity, for its basic premises, on which its values stood, were hypothetical and invalid. Christianity continued to spread until it engulfed the whole of the Empire.

6. THE DIVINE NATURE IS MANIFESTED IN ALL THE PROPHETS OF REVEALED RELIGION AND HENCE, THE REVEALED WORD PROCEEDS FROM THEM ALL

Thus, whereas Neoplatonism, with its principle of universal emanation of the divine substance, tried to show the ontological basis of revelation as a faculty common to all individual human souls, revealed

5

religion confined emanation, or manifestation, of the divine substance to the divine nature revealed in the prophets alone. But this divine nature, and hence, divine revelation, was not peculiar to any single prophet. It characterized them all, whether they appeared in the past, or will rise up in the future. And we find this principle explicitly stated in the Gospel, and in the Koran.

Jesus was often confronted by the Jews, especially the pharisees, on matters pertaining to doctrine. For example, on the observance of the sabbath, alimentary restrictions, and modes of purification. The Jews considered these observances as fundamental in the Mosaic religion, embedded in its revelation, and equal in authority and validity with it. If the Word revealed by the prophets were considered as the foundation, such interpretations given to it and the memorable traditions that had gradually been added throughout the ages were like bricks which had been securely based upon it. All together, the Jews believed, constituted the edifice of the Law, which was incumbent upon them to observe. As we have stated, Jesus rebuked the pharisees for such belief: for deliberately confusing tradition with the basic doctrines revealed by the prophets. Whereas he considered himself bound by the revealed Word and regarded his mission to fulfil its promises, he was uncompromisingly against human traditions and deliberately tried to abrogate them. To him, man was a creation of God, not an emanation of His divine substance. Hence, human traditions could not be confused with revelation or the Word, and be given equal validity and binding power. Throughout his mission, Jesus asserted his own interpretation of the Law, in complete disregard of what the priests, and commentaries, had established. And the principle according to which he acted was that the source of revelation and illumination resided in him as manifestation of the Word of God, not in the human interpreters of the Law.

Furthermore, according to the same principle and ontological ground, when speaking of the Comforter who was to succeed him, Jesus said: "But the Comforter, which is the Holy Ghost, whom the Father will send in my name, he shall teach you all things, and bring all things to your remembrance, whatsoever I have said unto you"(3). He also calls the Comforter "the spirit of truth, which proceedeth from the Father"(4). In other words, according to Jesus true illumination is in the actual words revealed by him, in whom the divine nature will be manifested. Just as he gave the true interpretation of previous revealed Words so will the

Comforter, or prophet that shall succeed him, give the true interpretation of the Gospel; for he also will be proceeding from the Father, and personify the "Holy Ghost" and the "Spirit of truth."

It was according to this fundamental principle, stressed by Jesus while speaking about the Comforter, that Mohammed said in the Koran: "O people of the Scriptures! Now is our Apostle come to you to clarify what has been hidden to you of those Scriptures"(5). In verse 48 of the same Sura, the Koran not only confirms past Scriptures but also asserts its own right to overrule what has been said previously. For it is only in the light of its own interpretation of the Word of God that past Scriptures can be appreciated. Furthermore, according to the Koran, revelation is imparted by God in the form of "Wisdom" through the intermediary of all the prophets of revealed religion, such as Abraham (6), Moses, Jesus, and Mohammed himself (7). Every one of such prophets explains and expounds, in the light of the "Wisdom" imparted to him by God, passages of previous Scriptures which are misunderstood, and give rise to contentions and divisions in the rank of the faithful. It is the authentic Word of God, revealed through these prophets, confirming, interpreting and expounding the truths of one another, which constitutes the source of illumination to mankind. Together they form the revelation of the primary premises human thought seeks. To put it in other words: authentic revelation proceeds only from the Word, the divine nature, emanating from God, and revealed in the prophets. That reality, put in the words of Jesus, "proceedeth from the Father," and hence, can be rightly considered the embodiment of "the Spirit of truth." The task of the seeker after truth is to study past Scriptures, unravel the truly revealed Word uttered by the prophets, read it in the light, not of human interpretations and commentaries, but of subsequent revelations of the selfsame "Spirit of truth."

7. WHEN THE PRINCIPLE OF EMANATION IS CONFINED TO THE DIVINE NATURE REVEALED IN THE PROPHETS, IT GIVES IT A CREATIVE CULTURAL PURPOSE, AND BECOMES AN ACT OF GRACE TO MANKIND

The principle of emanation, or "outflow" of the divine nature, is a sort of devolution. It cannot alone be creative and evolutionary. It is a mere division of fission, which must needs end in number if these purely physical processes can at all be applied to a spiritual reality, to elucidate its working. And that is what all mystic movements are led to believe, as an outcome of that doctrine, which they apply universally. For, what else does the "circling course of the divine life process" entail, when applied to the human soul, as the mystics did; that is, if it is regarded as a drop which has flown out of the sea of the divine being, and therefore, should pour back into it as its final destiny? In that case, no spiritual and cultural purpose is involved in the operation. It necessitates merely an ascetic life, a divesting of the human soul of everything earthly, of even cultural values, which are considered retarding forces obstructing its return to its original state. It implies a "fall" which only an ascetic life can repair. Cultural life on earth, would this be a thing to be transcended, rather than followed, served and improved.

On the other hand, if "the circling course of the divine life process," which involves the principle or emanation, is confined to the divine nature revealed in the prophets, then its operation becomes purposeful, evolutionary, and creative. Even though it might be a sort of "fall," or devolution, it will be an act of grace whereby humanity is reborn and made to acquire a spiritual and cultural life. For when that divine nature reveals itself in the prophets, and thus severs itself from the sea of its divine origin, it becomes the source of life to mankind. It becomes the means for man to learn the primary premises from which all his cultural values are derived. It becomes an exemplary of God's attributes of perfection, which man has to acquire, as part of his moral development. By reflecting those perfections it sets for humanity the standards of beauty and of the aesthetic life. In short, that devolution of the divine nature revealed in the prophets becomes thus the source of human salvation.

8. WHEN THE PRINCIPLE OF EMANATION IS APPLIED TO THE HUMAN SOUL AS WELL, IT LOSES ITS CULTURAL PURPOSE

If the human soul is also an emanation of God, proceeding from the divine being as an outflow, or projection, why should it still seek to acquire perfections? It already possesses them in the ground of its being as potentialities. Why should it seek to acquire knowledge and understanding of its environment, master its forces, and try to harness them to its use, if its supreme purpose is to transcend that environment, and divest itself of its fettering bonds? Why seek to acquire moral perfections, if it is

8

already in nature divine, qualitatively like God, though different only in magnitude? Why try to improve his social surrounding, and strengthen his ties with the rest of mankind, if man's spiritual salvation is in extricating himself from its entanglements? Why seek an aesthetic life, and make for himself a beautiful surrounding, if that adds to his worldly attachments and distracts him from attaining his goal?

The spiritual and cultural life of man can be real only if the principle of divine emanation is not made to apply to him, if his soul is considered as mere clay, and formless, subject to constant creation and regeneration. The purpose of knowledge, and understanding, would then be to set the goal of his evolution, and learn the nature of the forces which would help him attain it. The moral life would then be the process whereby he acquires perfections he lacks, but has the capacity to learn. His social surrounding would be that optimum environment in which alone his soul would find full scope to grow. His aesthetic life would be to stimulate his love and longing for what is truly divine. All these indispensable elements of culture become part of the purpose of its being; when the human soul is considered, not an emanation of God, but mere clay to be formed and reformed, reborn and regenerated, in its process of evolution, to an ever higher realm of being.

This principle does not possess only theoretical validity. It is what actually happened when we compare the cultural achievements of Neoplatonism with that of Christianity. The former remained a mere school of thought, which stimulated the growth of the ascetic life and became a theme for intellectual controversy, but did not influence the moral precepts that dominated Rome, or ameliorate the basic laws and institutions that prevailed. Christianity, on the other hand, left no phase of the spiritual and cultural life which it did not permeate and reform. Not only were the primary premises of thought changed; the moral, social and political life of the Empire was basically modified. From the private feelings and aspirations of the individual, to the administration of the Empire as a whole, every aspect of human life was remoulded, to conform with the teachings of Christ.

9. THE PROBLEMS WHICH THE DOCTRINE OF CREATION IS DEEMED TO PRESENT

Porphyry was fully justified in maintaining that the parting of ways between Neoplatonism, on the one hand, and Christianity on the other, starts with the doctrine of creation. For it actually begins with the theory of being and becoming; that is in both the ontological aspect, which each upholds in contrast with the other, and from it their respective systems branch off. There could be no more basic divergence more far reaching in its consequences. But in that intellectual controversy Christianity labored under a handicap not of its own making. Christianity, soon after its appearance, was made to subscribe, against considerable opposition from among its own adherents, to the literal authenticity of all which was recorded in the Old Testament, irrespective of whether they were revealed words of the prophets, or otherwise, that is, whether they were revelation proper, or tradition of men. The Book of Genesis stood out in the Scriptures as a faithful record of the process of creation. And Jesus had neither interpreted its true spiritual significance nor set it aside as tradition of men transmitted from one generation to another. It therefore stood as a valid record of what had actually transpired and this constituted the source of the handicap under which the Christian writers had to labour in vindicating the principle of creation.

10. WAS THE PROCESS OF CREATION IN TIME?

Of the problems the book of Genesis left unsolved one was whether the process of creation was in time. The main controversy between Neoplatonism and Christianity centered around this point. For, on the seventh day the process of creation is said to have ended, and God to have sought rest. Such a literal interpretation of the words of Genesis gave rise to insurmountable philosophical and theological difficulties. But was Christianity truly committed to such an interpretation? None of the ancient prophets of Israel stressed the literal meaning of those verses. Nor did Jesus uphold it. And if we follow the interpretation given to it by Baha'u'llah, we can conclude that revealed religion as a whole is not in any wise committed to it. In fact, revealed religion will categorically deny that naturalistic interpretation, on the ground given by Abdu'l-Baha, namely, if a God is infinite and eternal, His handiwork must needs be infinite and eternal. For any limitation to creation, either of time or space, would necessitate a limitation to the creative power of the Creator, a limitation none of the prophets of revealed religion would countenance. Therefore, on this point there is complete agreement between revelation, as vouchsafed by the prophets themselves, and reason, as upheld by philosophic thought.

11. WAS CREATION OUT OF UTTER NON-BEING, OR THE IMPOSITION OF A FORM UPON WHAT WAS FORMLESS, TO GENERATE A NEW INDIVIDUAL REALITY?

If the idea of creation, as an act done in time, is set aside, and the universe is considered as eternally existing, both in the past and in the future, then the process by which a new reality, out of non-existence, comes into being, should be differently understood and interpreted. For if we agree with revealed religion, that the world of creation has ever existed, and will ever exist, then there is no problem as to how this universe from utter non-existence came into being. Creation would then have to refer to specific natural phenomena and individual realities produced.

This point, of creation out of nothing, is disturbing only in the light of a definite system of thought which is basically rationalistic, such as that of Plato and Aristotle. For such a system identifies reality, substance, essence, and nature with definition, or the idea and form. And a basic feature of such an idea, or form, is that it is eternal and unchanging. So, the basic principle that a reality, with substance and essence, can come from non-existence into being runs counter to the basic tenet of rationalistic system of thought. And if reality, rationalistically conceived, cannot come out of nothing, they say, how can there be creation in that sense? Revealed religion, however, is not committed to the rationalistic theses to be disturbed by that objection. It maintains that the idea, or form, starts to be in the mind of the Creator; but then it has to follow a long process for its objective realization. Reality then resides in the object produced, which is individual, not formal. And this individual, from non-existence, came into being. That idea, or essence, is a mere form to be imposed upon an existant matter to constitute a real individual being. An idea is an intelligible reality. And an intelligible reality is inchoate objective reality. For an idea to become real, it has to proceed through a creative process that makes it objective. As the product of the creative process, it becomes a created object in the full meaning of the term. And when that being is thus created and substantiated it will have come as an individual, from non-existence into being. And the substantial reality of the individual is a point vital to revealed religion. Therefore, the objections of rationalism to the conception of creation is due to a definition of reality and to premises it has itself presumed and to which revealed religion is not committed. The formal definition of reality, and its conception as an

11

unchanging universal, preclude the principle that it can from non-existence come into being. It does not center reality on the individual and, therefore, denies that it has from non-existence come into being. The difference between rationalism and revealed religion on the subject of creation is the logical consequence of the difference of definition they give as to what constitutes reality: whether it is the unchanging universal form, or idea; or the individual object which the creator produces, be that object a physical thing or the human soul in the different stages of development.

12. WAS CREATION PHYSICAL, OR ALSO SPIRITUAL AND CULTURAL?

The third point raised by the account of creation given in Genesis is whether this generation is physical, or spiritual and cultural. If we discard the principle that the universe was created in time, and that on strictly religious and theological grounds, namely, that an infinite Creator necessitates an infinite creation, both in time and space, then a physical interpretation of the account is precluded. For there would be no such beginning to be accounted for. Hence, there remains the only other alternative, namely, a spiritual and cultural creation, or regeneration, of man in which religion is primarily interested, and for which prophets appear. And that interpretation of creation constitutes the one they have one and all given to it in subsequent dispensations.

As it proceeds, the Pentateuch develops into an account of how every recession of the spiritual life of the Hebrews was the occasion for a new act of divine guidance. That is the principle we can, for example, deduce from the story of Moses, and later of the Judges. At such recessions the earth was figuratively "without form, and void; and darkness was upon the face of the deep. And the spirit of God moved upon the face of the waters. And God said, Let there be light: and there was light. And God saw the light, that it was good: and God divided the light from the darkness. And God called the light Day, and the darkness he called light . . ."(8). The heaven and earth thus created were the spiritual and social elements of the cultural life. With the advent of every prophet of perennial religion, such a creative process starts "in time" as philosophy is wont to express it. The earth of human capacity is without "form," and "void," culturally and spiritually. And "the Spirit of God," revealed through the prophets, moves upon the face of the earth, which is steeped in "darkness," and sheds upon it its "light" of guidance. With that act it separates and puts in striking contrast the fast fading "night" of the existing cultural degeneracy, from the dawning "day" of spiritual life. Jesus, like Moses and the other prophets, appeared at such a turning-point of human evolution. He also found human capacities "formless" and imparted to them a new "form" and called that process of creation "rebirth." It was a creation, for that spiritual and cultural life from non-existence came into being. The rebirth was not the result of pre-existent earthly factors. It was a new state of being, willed and executed by the Creator, through the advent of a new prophet. Jesus was not concerned with physical creation. His task was the spiritual and cultural regeneration of mankind, individually and socially. For, "that which is born of the flesh is flesh; and that which is born of the Spirit is spirit"(9). And this spiritual and cultural interpretation of Genesis is the one adopted by Augustine in his Confessions (10).

13. THE TYPE OF PROCEEDING FROM GOD CREATION IMPLIES

A fourth point the account of Genesis raises is the manner the created proceeds from the Creator. And this, as we have observed, constitutes the basic source of difference between Neoplatonism, on the one hand, and revealed religion, on the other. Though Platonism was essentially dualistic, that is, distinguished and separated between the realm of ideas and the world of sense, mysticism was essentially monistic in that it maintained the existence of only one substance, that of God. And this monistic element remained dominant when the two were seemingly reconciled and incorporated into Neoplatonism. The object of mysticism was to give suffering man the semblance of deliverance from earthly uncertainties, to stress the unreality of his individual life, with all its passing interests and worries, and to ensure him of his final return, and submergence in the sea of divine Being with Which he was considered to be substantially one. But such a submergence in the sea of divine Being can be logically maintained only if the spirit of man be considered as originally springing out of the substance of God. An original substantial unity between God and the human soul could alone logically ensure their final substantial unity. Hence, it was fundamental for mystic thought, which Neoplatonism adopted, that there should prevail a substantial unity between God and the human soul from the very start. A drop of water should be in substance one with the sea, to become part of it again. There might appear a seeming temporary separation between the universal reality of the divine Being and the individual human soul, but in substance and essence they should be deemed one and the same.

Revealed religion, as we have observed, does not deny the existence and working of this principle of emanation, or we may term it manifestation; that is, of a projection or proceeding from the substance of God, in the manner of a ray from the sun, or a shoot from a stem, as the mystics are wont to express it. But it limits that form of projection, or proceeding, to the divine nature revealed in the prophets; for example to the Spirit of Christ which animated Jesus, and that as an act of grace, to establish the link between God and the generality of mankind. This projection, or proceeding, constitutes the ontological ground of their revelation, and the basis of their authority, as source of truth, to humanity. It is on this ground that Jesus said: ''Ye are from beneath; I am from above; ye are of this world; I am not of this world''(11). The Spirit of Christ, revealed in Jesus, as well as in the other prophets of God, is a temporary individuation of the divine substance, effected with the purpose of regenerating mankind. That Spirit of Christ, that Holy Ghost, or divine nature revealed in the prophets, is alone in substance, nature, essence and reality one with God. To put it in the figure of speech of the Koran, it is ''a star that has come low'' (12). The human nature of these prophets, the human soul of the individual man, objects of nature, whether rational or physical, none of these in any wise partakes of that divine nature and substance as mystics assume. These are not projections of the divine Being; they are merely the products of God's creative Will and Purpose, expressed through His fiat. And God said, let us make man in our image, after our likeness, and man came to be. And this process of becoming in the image of God, is not substantial, but qualitative: it is in the gradual acquiring of the attributes of perfection which are revealed by God through the divine nature of the prophets. When Jesus said: ''Be ye therefore perfect, even as your Father which is in heaven is perfect''(13), he did not mean that there was a substantial unity, and likeness, between God and man, nor that he will ever acquire it; but he meant that he can, if he strives, reflect the divine attributes of perfection in his soul. In other words, inasmuch as the human soul is not part of the divine substance, and hence, preexistent in It; that it does not emanate from God, but is the result of His creative fiat; that it is not a mode, or aspect, of the universal divine reality, but an individual substance; because of this we say that he has from non-existence come into being.

Action and reaction are signs of contingent being. An individual is what acts and reacts as a unity with the rest of the universe. The human soul is, as a unit, the result of the creative fiat, and will as such react to the revelation of His will and purpose. Its reality is not due to a universal principle residing in it: a universal and unchanging idea, or form, which is deemed to be the ground of its being. The ground of substantiality in a created and ever changing universe cannot be an unchanging reality but an ever growing and evolving one. The reality of the human soul is grounded in its individual response to the creative will and purpose of God as its Creator. In short, creation is not a devolution from a universal principle, as the doctrine of emanation implies; but the constant acquiring of an ever higher degree of perfection, and in conformity of the supreme divine purpose. This interpretation of the principle of creation, as acquiring perfections and training of human capacities was what Augustine upheld when he said: "For to Thee, being perfect, their imperfection is displeasing, and therefore, were they perfected by Thee, even pleasing unto Thee. . . ."(14).

If we thus follow the principle laid down by Baha'u'llah, that limitation of creation implies limitation of the creative Purpose, and hence, the limitation of the Creator; and that the infinity of the Creator implies the infinity of His creation; and thus set aside any limits to its extent and duration; in such a case the notion of creation will be confined to the generation and constant perfection of the individual reality, be that a natural object, the human soul, or a universal and universalistic society, termed "the Kingdom of God on earth."

In short, revealed religion has maintained, in contrast to Neoplatonism and other mystic movements, that emanation as an outflow of the divine substance and nature cannot be applied to all reality, but is confined to the divine nature revealed in the prophets. Hence, the world of nature, including the human soul, is a creation of God; in the sense that it is "made" by Him, and as other individual realities, brought from nonexistence into being. Therefore, whereas emanation, or manifestation, applies solely to the instruments of God's revelation, creation dominates the physical and spiritual being of man and nature which constitutes his habitat.

Baha'u'llah puts it in one of his writings saying: "Consider the

15

should be formal, and reside in the coherence of its different elements, or parts.

3. THE PRINCIPLE OF CREATION CONSIDERS TRUTH TO RESIDE PRIMARILY IN THE PRIMARY PREMISES

The principle of creation, in contrast to rationalism, is not formalistic in its interpretation of reality. To it form is merely a sketch for its creative projects. Its goal is the ontological generation of the particular and individual reality it seeks to produce. The formal aspect is, therefore, instrumental for its ontological and existential end. Hence, truth is not the product of logical deduction alone. The validity of a reasoning, if it is to produce the desired end, resides also in the efficacy of the primary premises, from which the logical deductions are made.

Creation, we have observed, is giving new form to an existent objective reality. It is to set a new definition, or limit, for an individual object, with the purpose of generating a higher one that would conform with it. The efficacy of the whole process, its truth, resides in the form, or definition, entertained and the logical deductions made from it and also in the end achieved. In other words, the efficacity of an ethical system of thought resides, not in the coherence of its deductions and the inner harmony of its different elements alone, but also in the definition given to the reality and destiny of man, initially established and from which the spiritual and cultural values are deduced as well as the results achieved in fact.

4. THE INTEREST OF ETHICS SHOULD BE CREATIVE:

The object of philosophy should be not only love and contemplation of truth but also improvement of the spiritual and cultural life of man: its regeneration. The object of Ethics, as one of its branches of study, should be the nurture of the human soul, and its guidance to a higher state of being. Neither should limit its field to epistemology. Both have to aim at the ontological aspect of man's individual and social life and being.

Being abstract, formal and universal in its interest and scope, mathematics can afford to disregard the validity of the primary postulates and the nature of objective existents. Its method is to deduce the consequences when such postulates are assumed, no matter what they are: whether real or fictitious, existents or assumed to exist. The objective validity of those postulates is not its major concern, they must be merely clearly and distinctly defined. Its task is to be logical in its deductions.

It should be otherwise with philosophy, if it claims to hear a spiritual and cultural mission that is of vital interest to humanity. The same is true of Ethics as one of its outstanding branches of study. Their object should be the ontological nature, and validity, of the spiritual and cultural life of man. They should not seek only inner coherence in their method of reasoning. Their goal should be to find the truth, and be not satisfied with their inner logical trend of thought. They should aim at the actual nature and development of that cultural life, and study the universal concepts, and the values derived from them, that would ensure the desired end. And to serve that purpose, philosophy and Ethics cannot overlook the nature of man and his destiny, from which these values are derived, and hence the objective validity of the primary premises, the ensuing process of reasoning, as well as the cultural effects they are bound to produce. In other words, Ethics should not be limited in its interest to providing a logical and coherent system of thought, but also in furthering the regeneration of the human soul. That should be considered the fruit of its investigations and reasoning and criterion of its efficacy. The purpose of thought is truth employed, goodness achieved, justice established, and beauty which is actually uplifting, and stimulating, to spiritual rebirth. It is the ontological validity and outcome of these values that culture demands from philosophy. Hence, the nature of those primary postulates is vital and foundational for attaining truth, and basic for a philosophy and Ethics that seek to promote the cultural life of man. They cannot, therefore, afford to maintain with Spinoza that "any hypothesis may be formed, provided only that it be clear and simple and that the phenomena of nature be made to follow from it by mathematical inference" ; that "there is no danger of error from false hypothesis"; that "the only which remains among all conceivable hypotheses is with the one from which all properties of a phenomenon may be deduced most readily"(1).

Such an attitude prevails to this day among students of natural science. Naturally by process of elimination, after due verification of all possible hypotheses, only the valid is deemed to prevail. But that procedure is too costly in the field of the spiritual and cultural life. Human life is too short, and the process is too daring, subversive, and detrimental to human weal. Man cannot afford to experiment with his individual, moral and social life and yet feel secure, eliminate fear, avoid recurring revolutions and wars and enjoy peace and prosperity.

19

5. THE PRIMARY PREMISES OF ETHICS SHOULD BE CERTAIN AND NOT HYPOTHETICAL

The primary premises of the spiritual and cultural life, namely, the nature of God and of the reality and destiny of man, should not be considered as postulates, or open questions, to be verified through gradual experiences; for, in the first place, they are by nature unverifiable. Secondly, such procedure, followed in the main at present, would constitute the source of uncertainty, as it actually does. It is, in fact, the major handicap under which social science is labouring, and which is highly detrimental to the spiritual and cultural life of man. The task of philosophy should be to eliminate it as far as possible, and thus avoid the consequences it entails. And it can achieve that by reformulating its postulates, and trying to establish them upon a basis which is certain and inspires confidence. And this is what revealed religion has offered to do down the ages. It has tried to impart validity and certainty to those primary premises from which human reason can make its necessary deductions. It is by shutting himself from that source of illumination that Spinoza suffers. The mere fact of giving his Ethics a geometrical form, with definitions, axioms, propositions and proofs, ensures Spinoza could not establish the practical and cultural efficacy of his conclusions, and render them spiritually wholesome and regenerating. To serve that spiritual and cultural purpose, his postulates had to be initially correct and his definitions regarding the nature of God, and of the reality and destiny of man, from which all cultural values are derived, had to be valid.

Spinoza admitted the need for some postulates, upon which the ethical life had to be built, and its thought developed. We are told that he "was convinced of the necessity of these postulates," that their denial "seems to him a denial of the whole efficacy of reason"(2). But the postulates which Spinoza chose as basis of all his reasoning were borrowed from ancient Neoplatonism and pagan thought; and that rendered his whole system pagan in origin and trend.

Truth, we said, is rooted in the primary premises, for these determine the nature of the objective reality, willed and purposed by the creator. If, therefore, the primary premises, assumed as hypotheses, are pagan in origin and nature, that is, they try to sidestep revelation, then that trend will remain the same to the end, in all the consequences it entails. The strictly logical process of reasoning and deduction, and its inner coherence, will merely bring out the necessary implications and make them

20

more obvious and certain. Because Spinoza's major premises regarding the nature of God, and of the reality and destiny of man, were pagan, and derived from ancient Greek sources, or sources which were themselves affected by Hellenic thought, his conclusions were of the same nature, and led to similar predicaments and cultural consequences.

NOTES

(1) The Philosophy of Spinoza by R. McKeon p. 116.
(2) The Philosophy of Spinoza by R. McKeon, p. 154.

CHAPTER II.

SPINOZA'S DEFINITIONS.

1. SPINOZA CLAIMS TO START HIS SYSTEM WITH GOD

Spinoza is said to have remarked to Leibnitz that, whereas popular philosophy begins with creatures, and the system of Descartes from mind, his own starts with God. But the claim is true if we take into consideration only his method of procedure in establishing the basic tenets of his Ethics. We should, however, penetrate further, and beyond this outward form and manner of procedure, to grasp the truth of his claim. To follow faithfully the method of geometry, Spinoza starts by formulating, in distinct and clear language, the basic definitions of the primary postulates of his reasoning. And the first definition is that of "Cause of Itself." He defines it as that "whose essence involves existence and whose nature cannot be conceived unless existing." (Def. # I) This definition is fundamental for Spinoza's system; for, as we shall observe, it constitutes the basis of his a priori proof for the existence of God. In fact, he considers that to be the only proof which is sound, irrefutable, and in full conformity with rationalism to which he subscribes. For its tendency is essentially a priori, and keeps clear of empirical considerations that involve elements of uncertainty. But does this definition of his basic postulate establish that his system starts with God as the absolutely paramount reality?

2. SPINOZA INDIRECTLY ASSERTS WITH DESCARTES THE PARAMOUNTCY OF REASON

Spinoza claims that his system of thought starts with God; but, in fact, like Descartes', it makes mind dominant. They both stand on the same pivot whereon all pagan thought rested, namely, that man is the measure of all things. For what does the attempt to define imply? It implies that human thought and understanding are the measure of the objective validity of that definition, that is to establish correspondence between the definition and the objective reality outside to be defined. To start with a definition of God is to begin from a conception we have of Him, an idea we already have of His nature, essence and being. And that is what we have already observed was the basic flaw in Descartes' reasoning. Man cannot define, without setting limits to the reality defined, without stating what it includes, and what it does not, without claiming the possession of a correct conception of its essence, or being, in his own mind. And this is all Descartes frankly and clearly claimed, but which Spinoza thought he was averting. In other words, before he starts with God as the source of all being and the origin of all thought, he makes God a knowable reality, and an object of human understanding which implies priority of the human mind. Furthermore, by saying concerning the "Cause of Itself" that "its essence involves existence, and whose nature cannot be conceived unless existing," he indirectly makes thought coextensive with its being, and that does not mean a relegation of mind to an inferior status.

3. TO KNOW IS TO DOMINATE

What man defines he limits: he states what properties it possesses, and what it does not. And a reality which he can thus delimit, discovering its properties and defining lines, he can find the means to coerce and control. To conceive the reality of a thing is the first step to staying its influence, stop submitting to it, accept its domination, or devise a method whereby its effects can be warded off. And a reality which can be thus defined, and hence delimited, with the possibility of dominating it, or at least of staying its influence, cannot be considered a "Causa sui," a reality which is unmoved Mover of the whole universe and of the spiritual and cultural life of man. Man can define what he transcends, or at least stands on level with, not a reality which far transcends him, a reality of which he is a mere artifact. Hence, God is undefinable and unknowable. This definition of Spinoza rests upon the faulty basic rationalistic premise which states that what man can conceive, that is real; that ultimate reality is in the nature of an idea, essentially knowable; that there is no province of being, inaccessible to human intellect and understanding. And this doctrine is in absolute contrast with, and contrary to, the basic

23

principle of all revealed religions, namely, that ultimate reality is essentially unknowable; that no man knows the Father, as Jesus said; that no human faculty can reach an understanding of God, as the Koran states.

4. THE BAB STARTS WITH THE PRINCIPLE THAT GOD'S ESSENCE IS UNKNOWABLE

All revealed religions start with the basic doctrine that the divine substance, and essence, are absolutely transcendent to human thought and being, and hence, are unintelligible and inconceivable. For that entails the need for revelation. It is because no one can know the Father, that the Son is sent to act as "light" and source of illumination, the "path" through which humanity can attain to the divine presence, understand and contemplate God's attributes of perfection, and learn of His will and purpose. Furthermore, "no man knoweth who the Son is, but the Father." For only He who dispatched the son knows his substance and reality.(1) Hence, the supreme object of human understanding is merely the attributes of perfection: the love, humility, wisdom and dominion which the human nature of Jesus manifested, when stimulated by the divine nature revealed through him.

The Koran starts with the words that God is "merciful" and "compassionate" which are attributes human understanding can grasp. It thus seemingly makes the supreme reality knowable and conceivable. But the verse proceeds to identify it with "the Lord of the Judgment Day." Hence, it can be identified, not with the transcendent divine essence, but with God's revelation, which constitutes the source of the spiritual and cultural life of man. It can be taken to refer to the return of Jesus Christ in the glory of the Father, as foretold in the Gospel. But this verse, which presents the supreme reality as the Merciful and the Compassionate, and the Lord of the Judgment Day, though it presents God as intelligible, and an adequate object of human understanding, is based upon the more basic doctrine, that in His substance and essence He is absolutely transcendent to human thought, that "no human faculty can reach Him." (2)

It is this fundamental doctrine, common to all revealed religions, which the Bab stresses in the opening passage of his Persian Bayan. He glorifies God, the supreme Being, as the "inaccessible," and "incomprehensible." No one, he says, has ever attained a knowledge of Him; or can possibly acquire an understanding of Him. Because of this transcendence and utter inaccessibility of God, He has periodically sent prophets to reveal His will and purpose to mankind. Through that act of grace and self-revelation He becomes the source of illumination which human intellect can grasp. In short, whereas Spinoza conceives God as object of definition and human understanding, and hence indirectly renders mind or reason prior, as Descartes did before him, the Bab starts his reasoning with a God who is absolutely transcendent to human thought, and hence prior to mind or reason.

5. SPINOZA WAS DOMINATED BY THE GREEK CONCEPTION OF THE UNIVERSE AND ITS CAUSATION

The Eleatics had identified "the One," or "the All," with the universe, and with God. They conceived it as unchanging and motionless; in utter contradiction of Heracleitus, the empiricist who saw a "flux" permeating all things. A compromise between the two views was to consider the universe as a whole motionless and unchanging, with its constituent parts subject to change. This change and motion were due to causal relations. As "the All" was so all-inclusive as to leave no reality beyond, it could not be considered as causally related to any other. It had to be considered as self-generating and causa sui. It was its parts and elements that were in flux and causally bound together.

Furthermore, the relation between "the All," or the Universe, and the individual objects of sense, that is, between "the One" and the plurality of beings, was considered to be numerical; that is, a difference of number and magnitude, not of qualities and form. It was the relation of a line with its segments. And such a conception of the process of becoming, we have already observed, was emanative, not creative. It is a segmentation of a primordial reality into parts, formally alike.

It is in the light of these two principles that the definitions of Spinoza have to be studied and appreciated. These views had circulated, and gradually been adopted and incorporated, in European thought. And upon them, as primary premises, Spinoza built his system of Ethics.

6. THE CONCEPTION OF THE UNIVERSE AS "THE ALL" IN THE LIGHT OF THE TEACHINGS OF THE BAB

In clear contrast to this pagan conception of the universe as "the All" adopted by Spinoza, we have the view of the Bab, who distinguishes completely between the Creator and the created. For, to bundle together these two realities is logically unjustified and conducive to grave consequences, detrimental to the spiritual and cultural life. How can we include the Creator and the created under the same category, and make that universal notion valid and useful? For the one possesses infinite and perfect forms to reveal, and the other the faculty to receive, and the capacity to acquire them. Can we identify the reality of Christ, who acted as source of illumination, with that of Peter, whose supreme attainment was to act as a clear mirror and reflect that light?

The Bab says that the fundamental tenet of religion and its system of thought is the verse: "I am God. There is no other God but Me. All others than Me are my creation. O My creation worship Me"(3). According to this dictum, the physical universe, including the human soul, is other than God, and hence pertains to the world of creation; and the two cannot be classed together and termed "The One." Further, in the opening passages of the Persian Bayan, the Bab states emphatically that "nothing resembles" God, "nothing stands as His equal," "nothing bears likeness to Him." "He has no peer," "He is and ever will be unique in His domain." If there is such basic qualitative and formal difference between God and the universe, how can we join them under "The All?"

7. "CAUSA SUI" APPLIES TO THE UNIVERSE AS CONCEIVED AND DEIFIED BY THE GREEKS, NOT TO THE GOD OF REVEALED RELIGION

Causation is a category of relation which necessarily implies a plurality of being. And that cannot be applied strictly to the relation between an absolutely transcendent creator and His creation. It can apply within the realm of the created only, between coexistents there. For only then can we say that alteration in one is accompanied by alteration in the other. The term "causa sui" does not avoid that pluralism; for it implies a plurality of nature or modes in the same reality. The Eliatic conception of God however, as "the All", would lend itself to such an expression; for it includes the intellectual and the physical nature of the Universe.

It is on this ground that The Bab states that "the eternal Substance cannot be correlated with anything"(4). And as there can be no correlation, there can be no causation as a category of relation. Referring to that divine Substance, he says elsewhere: "No act can be attributed to Him," that we should be entitled to say of Him that "He acts," or that "He

26

ordains'"(5). These expressions, The Bab says, would better apply to the Primal Purpose, which was generated by God to create all things; and in that case might be considered as related to all things. To "act" and to "ordain" imply a before and an after which "purpose" defines.

Thus, in revealed religion "causa sui" could be applied to the Primal Purpose revealed in the prophets, which is an emanation of the eternal Substance of God. For the Primal Purpose is in direct relation with the universe and the spiritual and cultural life of man as their creator, sustainer, and regenerator. Correlation demands a measure of contiguity. It is, for example, farfetched and remote to say that life on earth is dependent on the sun for its nurture; but we can stress that it is, for its rays. These are, in relation to plant life, "causa sui," for they are emanations of the sun and pure spontaneity in relation to the earth. The spiritual and cultural contiguity of man is with the divine nature revealed to the prophets; not with that absolutely transcendent God, which is neither perceived, nor can be conceived. The "causa sui," that pure spontaneity, the unmoved Mover, is the revelation of that imponderable reality. For it is that revelation of the divine Substance on earth, which constitutes His "Presence," and therefore is correlated with human society and can act as cause of its regeneration. That "Presence" renders the divine attributes of perfection objects of human contemplation and subjects of human understanding. In short, categories of human understanding apply only to the divine nature revealed in the prophets, which is within the sphere of understanding, as a source of universal grace to mankind.

8. "CAUSA SUI" MAY BE IDENTIFIED WITH THE PROPHETS AS FOUNDERS OF REVEALED RELIGION

Thus, only the pagan conception of the Universe, which, though considered divine, assumes the idea of magnitude, which is subject to division and fission, would admit the notion of "causa sui." Its essential duality of nature—of one and all—justifies its application. Otherwise it is inapplicable to the divine Substance as absolutely transcendent to all things. If we are determined to search for the principle of a "causa sui" in the field of revealed religion and within the reach of human understanding, and therefore, within the category of relation and causality, the only place we can locate its application is in the prophets as creators of the spiritual and cultural life of man. For, in the first place, this plane of existence is the specific province of human thought and understanding and hence, of the categories, and of causation. Secondly, it is the field where creation, and regeneration, as constant improvement is clearly discernible and intelligible. These establish mutual relation between the divine nature of the prophets, on the one hand, and the cultural life of man on the other. Thirdly, there is the element of spontaneity. For the message of the prophets, and their advent, are acts of divine grace, not outcomes of prevailing conditions in human society. Being a creative act, it is fully spontaneous. It is self-revelation.

9. SPINOZA CONSIDERS THE SENSIBLE AND THE INTELLIGIBLE LIMITED ONLY BY REALITIES OF THEIR OWN KIND

Like many of his contemporaries, Spinoza took some pagan postulates and made them the primary premises of his deductions. Among these was the principle of emanation which he attributed to all things. Intellect he considered to be the highest of such emanations and physical being the lowest. With this as postulate, he formulated the basic definitions of his system of Ethics. "That thing," he says, "is said to be 'finite in its kind' (in suo genere finata) which can be limited by another thing of the same kind—e.g., a body is said to be finite because we can conceive another larger than it. Thus a thought is limited by another thought. But a body cannot be limited by a thought, nor a thought by a body."(6) According to contemporary rationalistic philosophy, such a postulate, with such a definition, was fully justifiable. Geometry, which is the field of rationalism par excellence, and of which Spinoza copied both the form, as well as the spirit, in the formulation of his system of Ethics, maintains that an abstract figure is bounded, or defined, by an abstract figure, and abstract lines by abstract points. All these are abstract conceptions and formal, and hence, intelligible in nature and can limit one another. On the other hand, a physical plot of land, which is a body, is limited by other physical plots. Hence, thought and body each has its own realm and type of limits: form can be limited by form, and body by body.

10. THOUGHT AND BODY ACQUIRE REALITY WHEN COMBINED

This definition of Spinoza conforms with the doctrine of emanation for it conceives generation as division or addition of things formally the same. But according to the principle of creation held by revealed religion reality resides in the individual, for creation is of the individual. And the individual combines matter and form. Thought, or idea, or form, that is, the purely intelligible, is an abstraction of human intellect. When abstracted from matter, it possesses no existance and being. It constitutes an inchoate reality. It is a mere sketch, or project, for creative activity. It has definition, but no objective existence, or substantial reality. For it has no motion, and in a world subject to constant creation and regeneration, a substance must needs be active and moving. Similarly, body as pure matter, is an abstraction made by thought, for its specific purposes, which are theoretical. Thought and body, or form and matter, as existent realities, never stand apart and in mutual exclusiveness. They are always conjoined in positive, objective existence; for reality in a contingent world is of the individual, which comprises both matter and form. With such principle of creation, we can safely admit the eternity of matter; but it stresses the utter subjection of matter to the creative purpose of God. It exists only as the stuff from which the individual is formed. And in that capacity, it is constantly reincorporated to produce new individual beings. Other than God, the Bab says, is eternally in the baseness of its rank (7). And such created objects were composed of matter as a constituent.

If such be the case, then there can be no parallelism of thought and body, of each defining its own type. The human soul, through its faculty of thinking, dominates the body, and uses it as a mere instrument of its activity. Idea, or form, that is thought, is the factor which defines and limits matter to constitute the individual reality. Form designates the composition of the individual reality, states its type of motion, the direction of its activity, the properties it has, the purpose it is made for. All these are universals, and hence, formal, and are impressed on the body. It is true that an abstract, intelligible, geometrical figure is limited and defined by its sides, which are lines and points, that are also intelligible in nature, but the same is true of a physical body. The side-lines of all figures are formal in nature, even if they are physical bodies. The nature of all compounds is defined by abstract formulae. The motion of a body is defined by its direction and speed which are universal in nature and formal. And it is these forms which give the individual objects, or physical bodies, their properties, and define their functions. Even in the sphere of the spiritual and cultural life, which includes Ethics, it is the form that defines the beauty of a material object, and makes that physical body an object of art. Justice is a form imposed upon the physical and material relations of men. Goodness is a form imposed upon human activity. In all these cases the form, as an intelligible reality, a thought, defines or sets the limits and functions of the individual as body. To define is to limit the characteristics an object is to have, to designate its new function, direct its activity and set its purpose. And these are the role of thought, and applies to bodies. And because thought plays that role, and possesses that power, it dominates physical bodies, and can use them as instruments of its activity.

11. CREATION IS TO IMPOSE FORM ON MATTER, OR THOUGHT ON BODY, TO GENERATE A NEW INDIVIDUAL ENTITY

Creative activity is to impose a new form on a body, to give it new limits and definition. A mind is considered creative when it can generate a new idea or form, as a thought, and then impress it upon a body, to generate a new one, with new functions, purpose and properties. Deny thought the power of limiting and thereby defining body and the principle of creation as "improvement" will cease to have significance. Even geometry can have a creative aspect, and in that case thought is made to limit body and define it. For when we try to parcel out a certain plot, which has a certain geometrical configuration, and make different ones, in pursuit of a general scheme, we formulate certain figures in our mind, as thought, and then trace them on the plot to generate a number of individual ones in its stead. The process of that creative act is in imposing thought upon body to define its new boundaries.

We have seen the Bab emphasize the absolute qualitative difference between God as creator, and all other beings as created. But yet through His creative purpose He constantly and eternally generates new entities, by giving them new limits and definitions. Man is "finite in kind," but he is constantly limited and defined anew by his Creator, in his process of regeneration and rebirth. And this Creator absolutely transcends, and is far from being "of the same kind" as, the human soul.

12. SPINOZA'S DEFINITION OF SUBSTANCE AND ITS EMA-NENTAL NATURE

Similarly, the definition of substance which Spinoza presents us may be traced back to Greek thought, its rationalism and doctrine of emanation. It is that system of philosophy which provided him with the basic postulates upon which he defined substance as, "that which is in itself and is conceived through itself: I mean that, the conception of which does not depend on the conception of another thing from which it must be formed" (8). We can distinguish between three different conceptions and definitions of substance, according to the three main schools of thought; namely, the idealist, the materialist and the religious. The materialistic conception, held, for example, by Heracleitus, maintained that substance is in the nature of fire, and in constant motion and flux. The idealist, on the other hand, like Plato, stressed that substance was essentially formal, and hence, motionless and unchanging, which is its criterion of substance and reality. In fact, substance, the idealist says, is the reality which, through the motions observed in physical nature, retains its identity, and remains unchanged. In contrast to these points of view of the purposeless "flux" of the materialist, and the motionless conception of the idealist and rationalist, we have the definition of revealed religion which considers substance as a changing reality unit of matter and form, subject to an unchanging, dominating creative Purpose.

The Idealistic conception of all substance as unchanging can be easily traced back to the doctrine of emanation. For according to it, as we have already observed, all realities, other than God, proceed from His divine nature, as drops of water emerge originally from the sea. God was identified with the universe, or "the All;" and the human soul, as well as objects of sense were regarded as particles divided from Him, though in separate waves of emanation. The human soul was considered to retain formal, and qualitative, similarity with the divine nature. Hence, as the divine nature contained all the higher forms and was unchanging, the human soul also was considered to possess all the forms and need not move to acquire more. It was regarded as "unmoved" reality, moving physical objects of sense. But this immobility was not peculiar to the human soul; it was shared by the substance of all things. Objects of sense change, but their form, which was identified with their basic substance, remained the same.

13. THE DEFINITION OF SUBSTANCE ACCORDING TO THE DOCTRINE OF CREATION

The doctrine of creation, however, entails a completely different definition of substance, when applied to the world of creation, including

31

the human soul than when applied to God. The substance of the divine nature, the Bab says, is absolutely different from that of "other than God;" for the one is Creator and the other created; the one the unmoved Mover, the other the moved. And the latter being created, and constantly remade, and regenerated, is subject to constant and eternal change. That is true of units of physical being; it is also true of the individual human soul, which is constantly made to assume higher forms, and thereby, to rise to higher stages of being. According to Greek thought, all the higher forms are innate and ingrained in the human soul as potentialities, ready to be recollected as the occasion arise. According to the Bab, on the other hand, the human soul has merely the capacity (9) to acquire those forms, if adequately presented, and if urged and stimulated to practice and learn them. Because, in the first case, the forms are existent "potentially" in the human soul, no motion or change in its substance and essence is entailed. The knowledge of their nature and existence is mere recollection. On the other hand, because in the second case the forms are utterly non-existent in the human soul and this has merely the "capacity" to acquire them, through gradual practice and habituation, the process involves substantial and essential motion and change on its part. In other words, being subject to eternal and unceasing regeneration, the substance of the human soul cannot be, as the Greek conceived it, an unmoved mover. It is rather a reality which is constantly moving, and progressing to a higher state of being. It is not as Plato conceived it to be an unmoved captain of a moving boat; it is a child in the nursery, learning the way and aim of life.

14. THE NATURE OF SUBSTANCE WHEN CONSIDERED AS OBJECT OF THOUGHT

The definition of Spinoza approaches substance from a purely epistemological point of view, that is, it considers substance as an object of thought and understanding. It deals with it as "a conception," rather than an existent reality, forming part of the universe, and hence, ontological in nature. As a conception, the distinguishing feature of substance is that it is always subject, and never a predicate. As Spinoza puts it: "that which is in itself and is conceived through itself," and not through a quality, or predicate, that may be attached to it. Being "a conception," and always subject in a logical proposition, substance is considered to be formal in nature: unchanging and also supreme object of knowledge. Such was the attitude of Aristotle, for example, when he maintained in his Metaphysica (B.XII) that form has priority over matter as well as the individual object which is composed of matter and form in its substantiality. He admits there the possibility of considering either matter, or the individual object, as substance. He finds, however, that matter, though enduring, yet is object of sense perception; while the individual is both an object of sense and also perishable. And none of these qualities satisfies the requirements of rationalism which demands that substance should be both intelligible and unchanging. By such a process of elimination, Aristotle comes to the conclusion that form, which is both intelligible and unchanging, possesses priority of substantial being. In other words, he prefers the rationalistic definition of substance which is formal, to the materialistic one which considers changing matter as substance, and also to the creational one which attributes priority to the individual. And the reason for it is that only with the basic postulate that ultimate substance is intelligible, and hence, knowable, could his rationalism stand.

Revealed religion, however, denies the validity of this postulate, that is, the belief that ultimate substance must needs be intelligible, and hence, knowable, that intelligibility is criterion of substantiality. In fact, as we have observed, Jesus said that no one knows the Father; and the Koran states categorically that no human faculty can ever reach Him. Baha'u'llah proceeds further, and asks how can man dare lay claim to know the substance of God, when the substance of a stone stands as a mystery to him. Human thought, he states, is limited to the field of qualities and attributes. It can never proceed to the sphere of substance. In other words, revealed religion considers the rationalistic definition given by Spinoza utterly inadequate, for substance can never be "conceived through itself." Its conception depends on the conception of the attributes which it reveals and limited to them.

15. IN THE CONTINGENT WORLD OF CREATION, MOTION IS CRITERION OF SUBSTANTIALITY

Aristotle conceived God as the Form of all forms, drawing all things to Himself but Himself free from all motion of activity. He was conceived as the unmoved Mover of all things but not as a pure efficient Cause. He was a formal Cause as well, acting as the serene object of knowledge and contemplation. Such view seems in line with the cosmological principle which identifies the universe with God, for though itself stationary and motionless, acts as a centrifugal force, which binds the multiplicity of the world into one whole.

In contrast to this, we have the conception presented by the Bab (10), namely that, even though the divine Substance is beyond contingency and its change, His Primal Purpose is eternally active generating and regenerating all things. In other words the Bab does not, like Aristotle, identify the efficient and the formal cause of motion; he maintains a distinction between them, the importance of which we shall observe as we proceed. In other words, even though this Primal Purpose, an efficient cause of motion in the universe, is neither knowable in itself nor at rest, as a form or conception is, yet it constitutes the supreme reality that gives order to all motion in this contingent world.

16. CREATION IS THE SUPREME FORM OF MOTION

An undefined plane possesses the capacity of acquiring any geometrical figure a transcendent mind wills to impress upon it. These figures are not inherent and ingrained, in other words, immanent in the plane. They spring from the purpose the transcendent mind is pursuing. All manner of forms can be projected upon an object; but only certain specific ones can be taken in, and be impressed. All forms are shed upon all things. In some they reveal themselves as growth, such as in plants; or as spiritual and cultural evolution, which is peculiar to man. And this constitutes creation or regeneration.

Furthermore, the motion may be an activity, and of a positive nature, giving form to other than itself, and in pursuit of an intelligent purpose, seeking a desired end; or it may be mechanical and passive, merely submitting itself to that force. In either case, such phenomena imply the existence of an underlying substance; even though the one is creative and the other created; the one necessary the other contingent, depending for its very being on the first. Therefore, if an essential feature of a substance is that it is always subject and never a predicate, it is because in neither case it can be identified with the phenomena, or the qualities and attributes it reveals. The mover and the moved both have substantial being, even though the one imparts forms, while the other merely receives and acquires them; the one acting as a ray of light, the other as a mirror reflecting it. A quality, property or function is a universal conception, derived from repeated habitual activity referred to an individual substance. Because the motion appears as such a universal attribute, we predicate it of the subject as substance. It states the type of motion and behavior. The dependence of the predicate upon the subject, that is, the conception of the former, upon the conception of the latter, as Spinoza deemed it to be, is due to the ontological fact that the motion springs from the substance, or is directed to it. The predicate merely states the type of motion. In other words, the epistemological principle that underlies the definition given by Spinoza, namely, that substance is always subject and never predicate, is due to the ontological fact that motion is peculiar to substance, be that the mover or the moved acting as primal purpose, and hence creative, or subject to that constant regeneration, and created.

17. THE TYPE OF MOTION OF THE SUBSTANCE DEFINES ITS STAGE OF BEING

Furthermore, these different types of motion give rise to the difference between the strata of being, and are the ground of the priority of one substance over another. The Primal Purpose of God and of the divine nature revealed in the prophets, on the one hand, and of the human soul, on the other, both are existing and substantial because both are active and moving each in its own sphere, though one moves, and the other is moved. The one is active by its very essence and nature; the other is passive. The one is creative, the other is created, or at best, can participate with God's creative Purpose. The one generates the idea, or form, and imposes it as pattern on the other, to give it a rebirth; the other acquires it, and shapes its conduct accordingly, until it becomes part of its abiding characteristics. To use the example of the Bab, the one acts as the sun, shedding its rays of light; the other operates as a mirror, possessing merely the capacity of reflecting illumination. And the Bab stresses the fact that the light, the form or "image," as he calls it, resides not in the mirror, but in the reality from which it proceeds originally, namely the Primal Purpose.

But this principle is applicable within the world of creation as well, for how can we assign the same level of being to the human soul, which can participate with God's spiritual and cultural purpose and dominate natural objects and phenomena towards that end and other forms of life, which live on the level of mere sensation, and are fully constrained by natural forces? And how can we consider of the same class of being, an animal with full-developed senses and plant life, which is devoid of it or possesses it in a most rudimentary form? In all these cases, the nature of

35

the motion or activity, characteristic of that substance, determines the priority that reality possesses, and the stage of development it has reached.

But in all these cases, substantiality resides in the reality which moves, or is moved, that is, the individual, not the universal form that remains changeless. The form becomes objectively existent only in the individual moved. As a changeless form with an abstract nature, it cannot be considered as a positive objective entity, with a specific ontological reality, possessing functions, properties and qualities. Form, which is unchanging, acts as a formula. It designates a type of motion substance has or ought to possess. It would have to be an intrinsically moving thing to be part of this dynamic universe. It is true that the individual substance is neither intelligible nor unchanging. But these are criteria rationalism requires of substance. To revealed religion, neither of these characteristics are signs of substantiality. In fact substance is considered to be unintelligible and moving.

18. SPINOZA'S DEFINITION OF ATTRIBUTE IS CONCEPTUAL AND STATIC

In contrast to such a dynamic conception of the nature of an attribute, that is, of designating the type of motion the substance reveals, Spinoza says: "An attribute I understand to be that which the intellect perceives as constituting the essence of a substance." (Def. IV) To an observer, contemplating a reality from outside, an attribute is that "which the intellect perceives." But from the point of view of the moving reality itself, attributes are types of motion that it reveals. They are the habitual way it, as an individual, acts and reacts with other individuals within its sphere of operation. The perception of the observer is an accident of that activity, hence, it cannot constitute an adequate basis of that definition. What to an observer is epistemologically an attribute to the reality itself is ontological activity and motion. For example, the attributes we designate for God, as the supreme creative substance, are types of activity He reveals through His prophets, when acting as members of human society. Divine Wisdom is the efficacy and truth these prophets reveal in their words and deeds; His justice is the principle of social order and adjustment they exemplify when dealing with other members of society. His goodness is the exemplary life they lead. His beauty is the aesthetic value of their conduct. To God, these are types of activity, to an observer they constitute universal conceptions and characteristics.

19. SPINOZA CONCEIVED THE CREATED AS MODE OF THE CREATOR

Thus, in all these four definitions with which Spinoza starts his discussion of the basis of the ethical life, he follows postulates specifically rationalistic, which Europe had received as intellectual legacy from ancient Greece. His fifth definition takes up what is more mystic in nature and origin, which was also distinctive of Neoplatonism. It has its ontological source in the principle of divine emanation; for it is based upon the principle of unity of substance between God and the human soul and considers the proceeding of the latter, from the former, to be through the process of division. With that as a postulate, Spinoza defines "mode" as "the modifications of a substance or that which is in something else through which it may be conceived." (Def. V) It is, for example, through the nature of vapor, ice, and its other "modes" of being, that we can form a conception of the nature of water. It is through the surging waves that we can appreciate the sea. The ice, the water, the surging waves, and the sea, all are in substance one and the same. They differ only in appearance. As Jalaleddin Rumi puts it in his Mathnawi, it is only "color," or appearance, that distinguishes Moses, the prophet of God, from Pharoah, the arch persecutor of Hebrew religion. Only when subjected to "color," characteristic of life on earth, that these two seem in conflict. Transcend some way that "color" or world of appearance says the mystic, and you will find them both divine in substance and reality. Moses and Pharoah are here conceived as "modes" of the same divine substance. Outwardly they differ; inwardly and substantially, they are the same.

20. THE CREATED CANNOT BE CONSIDERED AS A "MODE" OF THE CREATOR

But in case there is unity of substance between the Creator and the created, they should possess similarity of attributes. Their inherent qualities should be the same. For the same substance cannot possess contrary characteristics one in itself, another in its "mode" one in the source, another in its outflow. Their motion and form of activity should be

37

identical in nature. A reality whose motion is to be constantly created and regenerated cannot be considered in substance one with the reality that created it. A substance which receives its forms as patterns of being, cannot be the same in nature with the one which imparts those forms. A ray of light, a shoot, a wave, as much as a musical composition, and an artifact, are objects proceeding from a higher reality. But the ray and the sun, the shoot and the mother tree, the wave and the sea from which it surges, possess the same substance in common, reveal the same properties, manifest the same characteristics and fulfil the same purpose. But we cannot maintain that there is such unity of substance between the composer and the music he has composed, or between an artisan and his artifact. And they do not possess the same kind of substance because the nature of their motion and activity is not the same. Their attributes, properties, functions and basic characteristics are wide apart. Such being the case, how can we claim the existence of substantial unity between God and the human soul, the reality of Moses and that of Pharaoh, and say they differ only in mode and appearance?

21. SPINOZA'S DEFINITION OF "MODE" WOULD APPLY TO THE DIVINE NATURE REVEALED IN THE PROPHETS

Substantial unity, we have observed, prevails, not between the human soul and God, but between Him and His revelation, namely, the divine nature revealed in the prophets. This is "the modification of a substance or that which is in something else through which it may be conceived." The divine nature revealed in the prophets may be considered a "mode" of God; for though manifest in the prophet, through it the divine nature can be conceived, and its attributes of perfection appreciated. This is the ground for the saying of Jesus: "Ye are from beneath; I am from above: ye are of this world; I am not of this world"(11). The divine nature revealed in Jesus, was in substance one with God, and therefore, "was from above." Man is part of the world of creation, and therefore, "from beneath." Commenting on the poem of Jalaleddin Rumi, referred to above, Baha'u'llah asks how can man identify the reality of Moses with that of Pharaoh, when the latter was brought into being by a Word uttered by the former, that is, when Moses was creator, sharing the divine nature of God? Mohammed compares the divine nature of the prophets to "stars fallen low." (Koran: The Stars).

The divine reality revealed in the prophets, and termed "Wisdom," "Logos," or "Primal Purpose," is the creator of man's spiritual and cultural life. It is the reality which gives man an ever new life and state of being. It constitutes the source of those forms, creative ideas, and values, man must needs acquire to be reborn, enter the higher realm of the spirit, and transcend the plain of mere physical existence. It is the reality, or substance, which integrates him into a higher individual being. How can we, therefore, maintain that this divine reality is essentially the same as the human soul, that the one is a "mode" of the other, or the two are different "modes" of the same reality? In short, modality can apply to the relation of the prophets with God.

Explaining the two natures the prophets possess, namely, the divine and the human, Baha'u'llah says: "The first station, which is related to His (the prophet's) innermost reality, representeth Him as One Whose voice is the voice of God Himself. To this testifieth the tradition (of Mohammed): 'Manifold and mysterious is My relationship with God. I am He, Himself, and He is I, myself, except that I am that I am, and He is that He is.' And in like manner, the words, 'Arise O Mohammed, for lo, the Lover and the Beloved are joined together and made one in thee.' He similarly saith: 'There is no distinction whatsoever between Thee and Thou except that they are Thy servants' "(12). The original Arabic word, rendered here into "relationship," is "halat," or "modes;" and that constitutes the bases of identity of substance and essence between the prophet and God Himself. This very principle underlies the words of Jesus to his disciples saying: "Jesus saith unto him, I am the way, the truth, and the life: no man cometh unto the Father, but by me. If ye had known me, ye should have known my Father also: and from henceforth ye know him, and have seen him. Philip saith unto him, Lord, shew us the Father, and it sufficeth us. Jesus saith unto him. Have I been so long time with you, and yet has thou not know me, Philip? he that hath seen me hath seen the Father; and how sayest thou then, Shew us the Father? Believest thou not that I am in the Father, and the Father in me? the words that I speak unto you I speak not of myself, but the Father that dwelleth in me, he doeth the works."(13) The very fact that Jesus could speak on behalf of the Father, that whoso saw him saw the Father, and that his attributes of perfection, are of the Father—all prove that the divine nature revealed in him is a "mode" of God, and in substance and essence one with Him.

39

22. SPINOZA'S DEFINITION OF GOD

We have already observed, while dealing with the definition of "Cause of Itself," that God is not a reality that man can possibly define; for his definition would imply that he is the measure of the reality and being of God. And though according to a rationalistic system of thought such an attitude would be inevitable, it is contrary to what revealed religion teaches. For this latter considers the creator to be the sole judge of the reality and being of the created. Neither the created can rightly claim to be the measure of the reality and being of the Creator; nor is he the person who stands as a mere observer, seeking to understand Him. Secondly, definition implies setting of limits and distinguishing between what is included, as properties of that reality, and what is excluded. Hence, it entails a comprehensive view and a measure of dominion over the object. This is the reason why Abdu'l-Baha states that only a member of a higher level of being can comprehend the reality of a lower, never that of a lower appreciate the reality of the higher. And the reason is very clear. We define an object only in terms we are familiar with. And the fact that an object belongs to a higher class of being implies that it possesses characteristics the lower lacks and for which it can have no terminology to conceive and express. Man can conceive the reality, and define the nature and properties of an animal; but never can an animal comprehend the power and capacities of man. Man, therefore, can never conceive God to define Him; nor would he possess the language to express that conception, and be able to articulate it, if he had any. To form a conception of a reality is to transcend it, at least in thought; to define it is to state its limits; and to appreciate its limits, presents the possibility of dominating it, and harnessing it in pursuit of a purpose. And this cannot be said of God.

Furthermore, cause is a category of thought applicable to creation, not to the nature of the Creator, whose eternal nature is unchanging. Hence, God may be considered as cause of "other than Himself," and not "Cause of Himself." This expression cannot apply to the religious conception of creation; but it may be used to express self-revelation characteristic of this doctrine of emanation held by ancient Greek thought. For, as we have observed, they tended to identify God with the universe, and consider individual beings as parts and particles of it. With such a conception we can maintain that God is "Cause of Himself." For the individual entities which compose it would be and move as a result of the forces which operate in its own being and maintain its organic unity. That internal addition and division, operating in the nature of the deified Universe, would be the cause of its parts. Such being the case, it is presumptive on the part of man even to attempt a definition of God. And this basic defect is observed in the definition of Spinoza that, "God I understand to be a being absolutely infinite, that is, a substance consisting of infinite attributes, each of which expresses eternal and infinite essence." (Def. VI)

To say with Spinoza that God is absolutely infinite, "consisting of infinite attributes," is not to state what those attributes are, of which we predicate Him. Hence, the definition is not meaningful, for it does not convey a positive conception of Him. To say of a reality that it is limitless is not to define it, nor say what it is and what it is not. It is in fact a negation of limitation, and hence, of positive definition. Therefore, it stands in absolute contradiction to what we would consider a "clear and distinct idea," which according to Spinoza himself, is the distinguishing mark of truth, which every definition ought to possess. Such a definition evokes merely a negative conception of God. It denies limiting lines. It does not establish any to define Him. It only asserts that God is free from those limitations that characterize the world of creation. And the reason for leaving out all positive attributes of perfection in his definition was, we might think, in deference to the spirit of Deistic thought which then prevailed in Europe. As Baha'u'llah states, "Confession of helplessness which mature contemplation must eventually impel every mind to make is in itself the acme of human understanding, and marketh the culmination of man's development."(14)

23. ETHICS DEMANDS A SUPREME REALITY WHICH IS DEFINABLE

This Deistic definition of God is correct so far as it goes, for man cannot fare any better in his understanding of the divine nature and Its attributes. It would have been more fitting, however, for Spinoza, as a philosopher, to disclaim any right on the part of man to define that transcendent reality. But the main difficulty is to find how, on such inadequate definition, can man build up an ethical system of thought, while his ethical, spiritual and cultural life necessitates an adequate definition of God as source of all values. That definition would have to be "clear and distinct," and establish the positive attributes of perfection we term divine. It should help man define what is truth, goodness, justice and beauty. For only with such attributes of perfection can that reality inspire love in man and become the object of his contemplation and worship. A conception that is mere denial of limitations, does not set a positive goal for human conduct, nor urge man to cultural development. In other words, the definition of God given by Spinoza is neither valid and informative nor can it act as basis for the spiritual and cultural life of man.

It is because God reveals Himself through the medium of His prophets and these possess a human nature which makes them part of human society that He becomes the source of the spiritual and cultural values to mankind. For the attributes He thus reveals, through the positive words and deeds of the prophets, are actually definable. In fact, no idea can be more definable, more "clear and distinct," than the idea of goodness, justice, truth and beauty these prophets have revealed in their life and teachings. For, besides being expressed, they were exemplified. The term, "infinite attributes, each of which expresses eternal and infinite essence," when predicated of the words and deeds of the prophets, as revelations of God, obtains meaning and significance. It bears no validity when attributed to the transcendent Essence of God.

24. INFINITY OF GOD'S ATTRIBUTES

Thus, Spinoza was dominated in his thought by postulates which, he tried to show, can constitute the basis for the ethical life. His definitions were formulated to express those postulates he had received as legacy from Neoplatonism and other Hellenic sources. He tried to establish them in a language that is "clear and distinct" as primary premises of his own deductive reasoning to prove their efficacy and adequacy in solving ethical problems which confronted Europe in that age. His definition of God was a restatement of the old Greek one; and to deduce from it an ethical system was to render it pagan as well. For the nature of a system of thought is derived from the primary notions upon which it is based. And an outstanding predicament of monism, which was Greek and pagan in origin, was the existence of physical being, or what Spinoza termed "body." It constituted a predicament because it was considered, on the one hand, in substance divine; and on the other, of a nature seemingly different "in kind" from "Intelligence," or "Mind," which was regarded to constitute the substance of God.

Spinoza's preoccupation as regards this predicament is revealed in the fact that he proceeds immediately to an "explanation," which attempts to clarify, and distinguish, between the conception of God, as possessing infinite attributes, and the principle of "finite in its kind" he defined above, and which applies to "thought" and "body," both deemed as in substance divine but factually different "in kind." In this "explanation," Spinoza tries to show that the infinity attributed to God cannot be limited by either one of the two "kinds" of modes; for that would be limitation, and not characteristic of an all-comprehensive reality which comprises them both as "modes" of His being. Thus, whereas in the second of his set of definitions Spinoza was apprehensive lest "body" should be identified with "thought," or the one made to imply the other, here he desires to make sure that God's infinity is not limited by either "body" or "thought," so that both may be regarded as mere "modes" of His being: a principle characteristic of his system of thought.

25. THE PREDICAMENT IN EXPLAINING THE EXISTENCE OF "BODY" IS ENTAILED BY THE DOCTRINE OF EMANATION

The doctrine of emanation entails such a predicament; for it has to admit the principle that "body" also proceeds from the divine substance. Being an intelligible reality "thought" would easily and logically lend itself to the belief that it is an "overflow" of the divine nature and reality conceived as Mind or Reason. There would be a similarity of nature, and of "kind", between human thought and God, if the divine substance would be presumed in the nature of "Intelligence," as both the principle of emanation and rationalism, incorporated into a single system of thought by Neoplatonism assumed. No difficulty would then arise as to how the one would spring out of the other as its source. The predicament is in explaining how "body," which is sensible, and not intelligible and hence different in "kind" from "thought," can also proceed from God as "Intelligence," and source of all being. For belief in an independent, self-sufficient, and eternal "body" would necessarily lead to dualism, and disrupt the monism Spinoza tried to establish. Therefore, he stressed in his "explanation" that the infinity of God should not be considered as limited by a reality other than "kind," but by a mere "mode" of His nature. "For of whatever is infinite only in its kind," says Spinoza, "we

43

may deny the attributes to be infinite." Hence "body," though not in the nature of "thought," yet does not limit the infinity and all comprehensiveness of God.

26. A TRANSCENDENT REALITY CANNOT BE LIMITED BY AN INFERIOR ONE

If the human soul and physical nature are both emanations or "modes" of God, and hence, one in substance and essence with Him; if the individuation we observe in them is the result of numerical division and their unity of their addition; and as a result their being is at par and equal, then the infinitude we refer to them is of the horizontal type, that is, it is in extent, not in kind. In that case, we should be on our guard, lest the infinity we attribute to God should not be impinged upon by matter which, not being formal and hence intelligible, differs from Him who is a pure Intelligence. Spinoza tries to deny that matter can limit the infinity of God, by stressing in a dogmatic manner that the infinity of God is "absolute," and hence, is not limited by what is other than Him in "kind." He fails, however, to state how, if God and physical nature are in substance the same, and unlike only in appearance, if the difference is only in the fact that "body" is only a mode of the former, the one cannot limit the extent of the other. Ice is a mode of water; yet they do limit the extent of each other. It is not sufficient to be categorical and dogmatic in our language and definition. An explanation has to be given that is adequate and satisfying. And only with the doctrine of creation such an explanation can be afforded.

We have already observed that a transcendent reality, such as the Creator, cannot be said to be limited by the extent of His creation. In fact, the infinitude of the Creator necessitates the infinity of the created. For a limited process of creation, in either time or space, implies a limitation of the creative power of the Creator. The same applies to "thought" when compared to "body," or to "mind" when related to "matter." Mind cannot be considered as limited by matter; not on the ground that they are different in "kind" alone; but because the one moves, and forms, the other; especially in the sphere of the spiritual and cultural life. The more dominating and creative mind is the less can matter or "body" limit its power. The vaster is the extent of physical being the wider is the field of mind to operate. In other words, under the doctrine of creation, the existence or infinity of "matter," or "body," does not present a predica-

44

ment, when discussing the infinitude of God, or of "mind." When the difference of substantial being is not numerical, that is, only in magnitude; but also formal and in degree of reality, and nature of its activity and motion; that is when God is considered the Creator of all things, even the human soul; and when human intellect is regarded as dominant, and mover, of physical being, then the infinity of the one, far from impinging upon the infinity of the other, actually necessitates it. In such a case, the infinity of the one entails the infinity of the other. Thus, if "mode" applies only to the Primal Purpose, that is, to the divine nature revealed in the prophets; the infinite magnitude of the human mind, and of natural bodies, merely express and confirm the infinitude of the Primal Purpose. They do not limit it.

27. TIME AND SPACE ARE CONCOMITANTS OF CREATION

Thus, according to revealed religion, the infinity of the Creator demands the infinity of physical creation. These two infinities do not contradict one another, they complement and support each other. The infinity of the one is based on the infinity of the other. Any form of limitation, whether of time or space, attributed to the created, would limit the creative power of the Creator. In other words, the limitations of the created, that is, of the human soul, and of natural bodies, is causal, and not spacial and temporal. They are created, sustained in their being, and stimulated in their evolution by a supreme Reality which is their Maker. That is the nature of their limitation. It is in form and function, not in magnitude.

As the Creator is absolutely unchanging, He transcends time and space. These are concomitants of motion, and hence, of creation and contingency; they cannot apply to a reality that is utterly unchanging. The gradual process of creation—whether of physical being, or of the spiritual and cultural life of man; whether of his individual regeneration, or of the integration of society into a universal Kingdom of God on earth, as an optimum, universalistic environment adequate for his growth—that creation necessitates time as a concomitant. That gradual creative process is the supreme form of motion and time is a necessary concomitant to it. Space comes into being when that creation is physical. Creator implies the created just as cause implies effect. But that should not be made to include the substance and essence of God, as Spinoza's principle of modality entailed. As Baha'u'llah says: "To every discerning and illuminated heart it is evident that God, the unknowable Essence, the divine Being, is immensely exalted beyond every human attribute, such as corporeal existence, ascent and descent, egress and regress.'' In short, neither the limitations of time and space, nor their infinity can impinge on the infinity of a spiritual reality which is in essence creative unchanging, perfect, and pure spirit.

28. THE PRINCIPLE OF EMANATION DISREGARDS THE REALITY OF TIME

The principle of emanation, the substantial unity between God, the human soul, and physical nature, it maintains, together with the idea of modality attributed to thought and body, all lead to basic predicaments, which the doctrine of creation avoids. The first and main predicament in the realm of ethics, is that it leaves no ground for the evolution of the human soul, and its creation in the sense of "improvement," and hence, of the objective reality of time, as concomitant of that motion. For if the human soul is already divine, possessing all the higher forms or attributes of perfection, already ingrained and innate in its nature, then there is no field left for acquiring higher ones, and "improvement." In such a case, time as concomitant of motion, and creation, would not be operative, or at least bear much significance in that process. And in contrast to this is the doctrine of creation which, through the process of "improvement" it maintains, attributes full efficacy to time as a feature of that progress.

The doctrine of emanation, we have maintained, is a principle of devolution while that of creation is of integration and evolution. It is of a reality generating an idea, pattern or form, and impressing it upon an existing object used as matter, to raise it to a higher stage of being. Mysticism, with its principle of emanation maintains, as part of the circling course of the divine life process which it advocates, that the human soul returns, and is submerged back into, the sea of divine being from which it originally emerged. It considers that process evolutionary and yet, free from the graduation of time. For the consciousness of that essential unity with the divine substance and being is sudden and instantaneous. It is like a sudden awakening to a truth. This conversion is considered to be as sudden as the awakening of man from sleep. The process has no duration or time involved. In other words, just as the doctrine of emanation does not consider the acquirement of perfection as involving a gradual process, so it does not regard the consciousness of unity with the godhead as demanding an element of time. In such a system of thought, time is a mere deception, an appearance, and unreality.

According to the doctrine of creation, however, time is an essential concomitant, with as much objective reality in the world of contingency as the individual objects themselves. For the motion involved in creation cannot operate without it. Creation is a gradual evolutionary process and the "improvement" of the individual, by acquiring perfections he lacks, and of society in which he has to be reared into physical, cultural and spiritual maturity, all demand time. In other words, when forms are considered as existing potentially in the human soul, their actualization does not demand time. It is a sudden awakening and reminiscence of its existence. But when the soul is considered as possessing merely the capacity of acquiring those forms through constant practice, and gradual habituation, then the element of time is unavoidable. A child has to have time to accumulate knowledge and understanding, as well as to acquire healthy habits of behavior.

The same principle applies to the social evolution of man. The prophets of Israel, and Zoroaster, foretold the advent of the Kingdom of God on earth as a future eventuality, when a state of universal peace and brotherhood will prevail. And they visualized that supreme event at a time when humanity was still in its tribal stage. They considered that day to dawn, after a long lapse of time, after several cycles of prophetic dispensations that will serve the realization of that divine purpose. This involved a long process of social development which necessitated time as a concomitant. It entailed centuries of constant endeavour and spiritual and cultural advancement.

29. SPINOZA'S DEFINITION OF FREEDOM AND NECESSITY

"That thing is said to be free," says Spinoza, "which exists by the mere necessity of its own nature and is determined in its actions by itself alone. That thing is said to be necessary, or rather compelled, when it is determined in its existence and actions by something else in a certain fixed ratio." (Def. VII) The principles of freedom and of necessity can be similarly interpreted, that is, either in the light of the doctrine of emanation, as held by Spinoza, or in accordance with that of creation, advocated by revealed religion. "Thought" and "body," that is, the human soul and physical being, both are considered by Spinoza emanations of

47

God, and divine in substance. These are regarded as mere "modes" of the universal divine Reality and Essence. To use the figure of speech used to explain emanation, the individual soul, or body, is a mere shoot of that universal and eternal tree, or a ray of light shed by the sun. The individual shoot, or ray, is, and continues to be, of the same kind and organically united with the tree, or the sun. Therefore, it is subject to the laws that dominate the inner functioning of the whole. That law may coerce the different members to work together, and thereby deny them any freedom of activity but in so far as the organism as a whole is not compelled it should be regarded as free. For that necessity is of its own nature and it is determined in its actions by itself alone. As part of the universal substance of God, therefore, the individual human soul is free, so is every other individual object of nature. This is exactly the same type of definition Stoics as Pantheists and upholders of the doctrine of emanation gave to freedom. For even if the human soul and objects of nature are seemingly compelled by the laws of nature in their activity, those laws are "mere necessity of its own nature," of the divine substance of which they are "modes" of being. With the primal premise of identifying God with nature and the human soul, this conclusion is the only logical deduction.

But can there be a true field of freedom under the doctrine of emanation? What does freedom actually imply when attributed to a universal reality? Can the whole of being desire anything when there is no reality beside and beyond itself? And if there is nothing it wishes, what is the purpose or meaning of that freedom? In fact, such a conception of freedom can be used to justify the regimentation of the individuals denying them the most elementary forms of liberty of choice and trying to make them contented with their lot and satisfied with their personal subjugation. This is exactly what the Stoics preached in ancient days to slaves and to those who felt the exacting burden of Roman rule.

To attribute freedom to that universal and all-comprehensive reality is a worthless lip service to and compromise with the religious belief that God is necessarily free. It is a meaningless and perhaps harmful yielding to a fundamental religious notion, indispensable to the spiritual and cultural life. If the individual human soul emanates from God's substance, as a shoot springs out of a tree, or a ray of light radiates from the sun, where does the freedom of that all-comprehensive reality reside? If it is "by the mere necessity of its own nature," why should we call it free? The idea that it is a characteristic of God's substance does not render that process free. There can be no alternative choice for that devolution to make it free at least in the sense which we ordinarily attribute to that term. Does the emanation of light imply freedom on the part of the sun; or the overflow of a river from its source entail liberty?

Secondly, if the individual is, as the doctrine of emanation conceives him, a microcosm containing potentially all the forms inherent in the universe as a macrocosm, what freedom of choice is presented to him? Is the possession of those forms the result of a freedom of choice? Was the slave boy, in Plato's *Meno,* confronted with any freedom when reminded of the forms ingrained in his soul? The principle that man possesses potentially all the forms ingrained in his soul and has merely to be reminded of them to become conscious of their existence, obviates the need for freedom. Freedom of choice appears when the human soul has merely the capacity of acquiring them, or disregarding them completely.

30. EVEN IN RELIGION NO FREEDOM IS MAINTAINED WHEN THE PRINCIPLE OF EMANATION OPERATES

We have maintained that the divine nature revealed in the prophets is an emanation of the substance of God, that it is an effulgence of His light, shed upon the human nature of the prophet, acting as a mirror. But then no freedom is claimed by them on that ground. In fact, one and all they constantly stress the compelling power of God in the pursuance of all they say and do. The supreme task of the human nature in Jesus, for example, was to operate as a pure channel for the divine nature in him—a nature which, having come out of God (15), as an emanation of His reality and substance, was one with Him (16). Identifying "the Son" with the divine nature in himself, Jesus said: "Verily, verily, I say unto you, The Son can do nothing of himself, but what he seeth the Father do: for what things soever he doeth, these also doeth the Son likewise"(17). "I can of mine own self do nothing: as I hear, I judge: and my judgment is just; because I seek not mine own will, but the will of the Father which hath sent me"(18).

Speaking in the same trend of himself, Mohammed says: "Your companion does not err, nor is he led astray. It is a revelation revealed, taught by the All-compelling power......"(19). Similarly Baha'u'llah says: "I have no will but Thy will, O my Lord, and cherish no desire except Thy desire. From my pen floweth only the summons which Thine own exalted pen hath voiced, and my tongue uttereth naught save what the Most Great Spirit hath itself proclaimed in the kingdom of Thine eternity. I am stirred by nothing else except the winds of Thy will, and breathe no word except the words which, by Thy leave and Thine inspiration, I am led to pronounce''(20). And it is because the prophets are such empty reeds that the divine reality in them which is an emanation of God, and one with Him in substance and essence, can breathe its word, will and purpose, and fully reveal the divine attributes of perfection. Between the creator and his primal purpose there is no ground for freedom to appear.

31. FREEDOM AND CAUSALITY ARE INTER-RELATED, AND THEIR FIELD OF OPERATION IS THE WORLD OF CREATION

Just as much as causation is inapplicable to the inner nature of God which is unchanging, and hence, transcendent to such principle of relation, so freedom cannot be referred to it. Once a reality is absolutely transcendent to thought and contingency we cannot apply to it categories that are essentially contingent in nature and imply it. Furthermore, freedom and compulsion, like causation, imply a duality which the unity of God's substance and revelation cannot admit. How can there be in the divine nature, which is unchanging, a field for causation? And if there can be no causation there can be no compulsion of freedom from it. Freedom, therefore, can have no sphere of operation under the doctrine of emanation, where the principle of substantial unity between God and the human soul is maintained. Freedom operates only when there is no such substantial unity implied, when there can be a cause and an effect, an element of compulsion, and hence, a possibility of freedom of judgment and activity. Only as Creator can we say of God that He is free to create, and man free to abide by His will and purpose, or rebel. In other words, only a ''Mover'' is free to move a reality; and only a ''moved'' can possess the faculty to resign to it or refuse. In short, freedom pertains to the spiritual and cultural creation, or regeneration, of man. It is based on the contingency of his moral and spiritual evolution.

32. THE FIELD OF FREEDOM IS THE SPIRITUAL AND CULTURAL LIFE OF MAN

We have throughout maintained that the object of revealed religion is the evolution of the spiritual and cultural life of man. The outstanding

50

feature of this evolution is the periodic appearance of prophets to reinterpret the fundamental notions and restate the primary premises and precepts of that perennial religion. It is to infuse it with new vigor, vitality and determination. In the Bayan, the Bab repeatedly states that, at the appearance of every one of these prophets, man is confronted with an alternative: either to accept that prophet, dedicate his life to the realization of God's creative purpose for mankind, and thus be counted of "the exalted," and of people of "affirmation," or to deny him, seek to obstruct his cause, and be numbered among the "non-exalted," and people of "negation" and perdition. This is a free choice presented to every member of society down the ages and upon it rests his spiritual and cultural evolution. This faculty of freedom is imparted by the Creator, as a feature of His creation of man and its purpose is to make his spiritual and cultural life the result of full knowledge, understanding, and free participation in God's design.

The appearance of the prophets periodically, is according to an eternal law and order, that is universal and unchanging. It is absolutely necessary and compelling: otherwise God's creative purpose will be frustrated, and human spiritual and cultural life will fail. But within that framework of compulsion, necessity and pre-determined law and order, man is given personal freedom: either to partake of that creative life, further that divine purpose, and thereby, fulfil, his destiny, or to try and obstruct the realization of that ideal, attempt to frustrate the hope of the prophets, and be thereby counted of the people of "negation," and evil design.

33. THE CREATOR IS FREE IN THE PURSUIT OF HIS CREATIVE PURPOSE

Let us first consider creation from the point of view of the Creator, that is when he utters His fiat and says: let there be, and lo! it is. Such a creator, whether he be divine, or human, first conceives an idea or form. In this initial step he is free. He is free in his choice of that type of idea as a pattern, and project, for his design. He is also free in his desire to realize it. There is no compulsion exerted from outside upon the mind of the creator, otherwise he is not an unmoved mover. As Baha'u'llah expresses it in his *Hidden Words*: God felt urging love for man, and therefore, created him. It is an inner impulse and love that impels the creator to create. But a love that is coupled with knowledge and understanding. The creator is also free in his choice of the material to be used for the realization of that creative purpose. As the Koran puts it, that is a divine guidance: He guides whomsoever He wishes (21). There was no compulsion exerted on God to choose the Hebrews, who at that time were a lowly people, and make them instruments of His creative cultural purpose in the world. And when, after few generations, these ceased to be universalistic in outlook and righteous in their ways, wholly dedicated to the task they were chosen to fulfil, God was free to revoke the Covenant He had made with them, disown them, and choose another people, as Isaiah definitely states. It was through a free choice that God selected then the Zoroastrians, to carry on that cultural task in the world. And when, after a time, these also ceased to act as selfless instruments of God's cultural purpose, He was free to discard them and designate the Christians to undertake the pursuit of that purpose. In every case, there was no unconscious automatic overflow of the divine Being. There was an intelligent love for humanity, for the rebirth of mankind: a free choice of the means and end. And whenever that "chosen people" ceased to pursue that purpose and act according to the covenant they had made with God and became, as Jesus expressed it, a salt that has lost its savor, God felt free to choose another people in its stead, and make His covenant with it. In short, God, as unmoved Mover, is absolutely free: free in the creation of the individual life of man, free in His desire to rear him gradually in His own image, and also free to create the Kingdom on Earth, as the social and political environment, in which that individual is to achieve his salvation, and partake in the salvation of the rest of mankind. But this divine creative activity, though an absolute reign of law and order, leaves ample room for freedom to man: to pursue that cultural purpose, and make that life, at least partly, the direct fruit of his own free choice and creative activity.

34. FREEDOM IS TO THE EXTENT MAN PARTICIPATES IN CREATION

Every created reality is clay in the hands of its creator as artisan. He molds it as he desires, and gives it the form he chooses. Man is such clay in the hands of its Maker, with the exception that he has been given a restricted sphere of his own, wherein he can employ his creative genius. That sphere is the field of culture and spiritual development which distinguishes him from all other created beings and raises him high above them. But here also man is not absolutely free. Even here, as already observed, his freedom is restricted within the bounds of God's spiritual and cultural Purpose. Were the individual given full freedom in directing his spiritual and cultural life he would gradually revert to his natural and physical tendencies, and completely forget the high destiny for which he was made. On the other hand, were he to be fully constrained, there would remain no virtue in his activities. He would cease to be creative. For virtue necessitates a vision of what is good, just, true and beautiful, an understanding of what they imply, a free desire to attain them, and a knowledge of the means to it. As a result, we have, on the one hand, the eternal and unalterable law of prophetic cycles, to which humanity is subjected and on the other hand, that freedom accorded to man, to embrace their Cause and follow their way, or disregard them, and withstand its consequences.

The Koran states that creation pertains to God alone (22). The Bab reiterates the same principle in the Bayan (23). In other words, creation is the realization of God's Primal Purpose. And the supreme form of it is in the field of the spiritual and cultural life of man. Hence, we cannot consider creative that which leads to human perdition. Thought cannot be creative when based upon wrong assumptions and faulty premises as to the nature and destiny of man. The moral life is deemed creative when man is thereby led to acquire attributes that are divine. To put it in the language of the Bab, it is creative when it makes man of the "exalted," not of the "non-exalted," and of the forces of "negation." Man is creative when he serves the establishment of the universalistic Kingdom of God on earth not when he obstructs its realization by stressing class and national distinctions and petty loyalties which breed estrangement and war. In short, it is in the cultural field of creative activity that freedom prevails. It is realized to the extent man submits his will to God's creative Purpose and reign of law and order, the extent he visualizes God's purpose and proceeds to realize it. To resign to the forces of "negation," which lead inevitably to spiritual and cultural degeneracy, is not the way of creation or of freedom. It is resignation to his disintegrating forces of nature.

35. THE SPIRITUAL AND CULTURAL LIFE OF MAN IS THE RESULT OF DIVINE GUIDANCE NOT OF COERTION

The law and order which governs the prophetic cycle was compared in the Scriptures to the laws of the Medes and Persians which were absolute and unalterable. It is as unalterable as the seasonal changes, when God "quickens the earth after its death"(24). In this respect, the Koran says, "Thou shall not find any change in the law of God"(25). This cyclic law dominates the spiritual and cultural life of man, puts a limit to the trend of his self-inflicted degradation and destruction and thereby restricts the field of human freedom, and its possible evil consequences. There is no people, the Koran says, to which a prophet has not been sent to warn and admonish it (26). The task of these successive divine revelations, throughout the history of mankind, has been to "warn" the people, "guide" them in the way of virtue and righteousness, and bear to them the "glad tidings" of the coming Kingdom of God on earth. In other words, even though the coming of these prophets has been "necessary," that is, subject to a "compelling" cyclic law of God, which is unalterable, their dispensation has been to "warn," "counsel," and "guide"; not to coerce. And warning, counsel, and guidance imply freedom on the part of man—a freedom that is coupled with knowledge and understanding. Jesus did not "compel" his disciples to arise, forsake all, and serve his cause. He did not coerce them to discard Roman and pagan values and follow his own. In fact, it was the prevailing "negative" forces which "compelled" the Romans to disregard Christian values, and follow the pagan ones. The early Christians asserted their right to be free in their choice, and flouted Roman authority. They preferred to follow the simple guidance given by Christ. They were free agents asserting their freedom, in the creative work they had undertaken. They were detained by no "compelling" prejudice, no obstructing preconceived idea, no fettering human institutions and loyalties, no social bond, no dominating political allegiance. They were moved solely by their inner convictions, attained through a freely acquired knowledge and understanding that the values proffered by Jesus were supreme. They accepted that guidance, in preference to the "compelling" forces which then pervaded Roman and Jewish society, and withstood persecution and death in that path.

36. EFFICIENT CAUSE IS "COMPELLING," FORMAL CAUSE PERMITS FREE CHOICE

We said that every created reality is "clay" in the hands of its creator. But that is the case only if the creator is considered to be the efficient cause of its being, and of the form it has assumed. For the efficient cause leaves no room for freedom to the effect. The latter is completely constrained. That is why on this level of nature there is no freedom of choice. But in the spiritual and cultural life of man, the direct cause of his evolution is merely the revelation of the efficient Cause, or the transcendent God. It is His revelation, or manifestation, as a Formal Cause, which we have identified with the divine nature of the prophets, that moves the spiritual and cultural life of man. The distinctive feature of a formal cause is that it is not an agent of "compulsion," but a center of attraction, that is, of guidance. Jesus Christ was not a source of compelling force but an object of clear understanding that stirred admiration and love. As formal Cause of man's spiritual and cultural life, these prophets reveal God's attributes of perfection, tell mankind the purpose for which they have been created and the nature of their spiritual reality. They set the example of godliness, trace thereby the road to their destiny, designate the means to attain it, and also prescribe the institutions that will help them reach that goal. All these are "counsels," "admonitions," "guiding principles," and "examples" for human behavior, which leave full freedom to the individual to follow or ignore them. "He Who is the Day Spring of Truth," Baha'u'llah says, "is no doubt fully capable of rescuing from such remoteness wayward souls and of causing them to draw nigh unto His court and attain His Presence. 'If God had pleased He had surely made all men one people.' His purpose, however, is to enable the pure in spirit and the detached in heart to ascend, by virtue of their own innate powers, unto the shores of the Most Great Ocean, that thereby they who seek the Beauty of the All-glorious may be distinuished and separated from the wayward and perverse"(27).

The Koran says that, had God willed it, His fiat will have converted all mankind to His Faith. He will have "compelled" them to embrace it. "What!" says Mohammed, "do thou desire to compel people to become believers?"(28) His, like that of Jesus before him, was the way of "guidance" and free choice, not of coercion. In short, all creation is under the compelling power of God. He makes it run its course, under a prescribed law and order, which is necessary and unflinching. Man alone was given to eat from the tree of knowledge and understanding, that is, presented with a vision of his destiny, and the perfections he has to acquire. That knowledge and understanding permits him a free choice. He may use it to his own detriment but he may also follow the guidance given him by God through the prophets, and employ it in acquiring those virtues.

37. THE CONTINGENCY OF MAN, AND HIS SPIRITUAL AND CULTURAL LIFE

"I understand eternity" says Spinoza, "to be existence itself, in so far as it is conceived to follow necessarily from the definition of an eternal thing." Spinoza establishes this definition, like the previous ones, upon the doctrine of emanation, as the only form of proceeding from God as universal Being, "the All" of Greek thought. In it he identifies existence with eternity for their conception imply one another. But through such identification, he limits existence to what is eternal, for he considers eternity to "follow necessarily from the definition of an eternal thing." This identification, or restriction of existence to the sphere of the eternal, or unmoved, limits existence to what is absolute, and excludes what possesses contingent being, that is, the world of creation. For, he adds in his explanation that it "cannot be explained by duration or time"; and these we have said, are essential characteristics of what is in motion. Where there is creation, there is motion, and that entails time and duration as its concomitant. In other words, Spinoza limits existence to the Mover who is changeless, and excludes what is contingent in being, created, and hence, moved. He limits it to what proceeds through the process of emanation, and denies it to what proceeds through that of creation.

In the Bayan the Bab states that the fundamental doctrine underlying all thought is the principle: "I am God; there is no other God but Me. All other than Me, are My creation. O My creation worship thee Me"(29). This primal premise necessarily entails that, "other than Me," that is, the world or creation, possesses objective existence. They were brought into being by the Primal Purpose. Though the human soul is immortal, and hence everlasting, it is not eternal. Because, being other than God, it had its beginning in the creative fiat of the Primal Purpose. It is moved, like all other objects in the world of creation. Furthermore, this creation, according to the Bab, implies birth, or coming into being; rebirth, or acquiring an ever higher form; food or sustenance; and lastly death, or proceeding to a higher stage of being (30). All these are fundamental phenomena of human life that imply existence, though of a contingent nature. Hence, they involve the principle of time and duration as concomitants of motion; and therefore, according to Spinoza cannot involve eternity of being. In short, according to the doctrine of creation, we cannot identify existence with eternity. God alone is both eternal and existent in the sense of unchanging. All other than Him, are brought into being, and hence, existent; but yet not eternal.

38. ONLY RELATIVE TO THE ABSOLUTE EXISTENCE OF GOD, THE CREATED IS NON-EXISTENT

Representing the point of view of revealed religion Baha'u'llah states in one of his prayers: ''......should any created thing lay claim to any existence, when confronted with the infinite wonders of Thy Revelation, so blasphemous a pretension would be more heinous than any other crime in all the domain of Thine invention and creation. Who is there, O my Lord, when Thou revealest the first glimmerings of the signs of Thy transcendent sovereignty and might, hath the power to claim for himself any existence whatever? Existence itself is as nothing when brought face to face with the mighty and manyfold wonders of Thine incomparable Self''(31).

In this passage, Baha'u'llah distinguishes between absolute existence, attributed to the unmoved Mover, or Creator, and the contingent existence of the moved and created. The one is like the effulgent sun, the other is like the visibility objects obtain when illumined by it. They are not comparable. In the sphere of the spiritual and cultural life, how can we compare the divine nature revealed in the prophets, with the reality of the human soul? The one is unmoved Mover, the other moved wholly by It. The one imparts existence, the other receives it, and is formed by it. In another prayer Baha'u'llah says: ''Glory be to Thee, O my God! The power of Thy might beareth me witness! I can have no doubt that should the holy breaths of Thy loving-kindness and the breeze of Thy bountiful favor cease, for less than the twinkling of an eye, to breathe over all created things, the entire creation would perish, and all that are in heaven and on earth would be reduced to utter nothingness''(32).

Leaving aside for the moment, physical being, including that of man, can the spiritual and cultural life be constantly reborn, sustained in its gradual growth, and thus evolve, if not for the repeated rebirth and regeneration it receives at the hands of God, through the intermediation of His successive line of prophets? Remaining on the plane of nature means that human thought will be essentially naturalistic and materialistic; that the moral life will tend towards satisfaction of animal instincts and natural desires; that brutal force will dominate social life; and the strong will make his will law. The spirit of man, and his cultural growth, will not be given full consideration; nor its needs made the object of diligent study and social planning. The aesthetic life will lose its uplifting and spiritualizing force by becoming subject to physical and sensual considerations. In short, it is through the creative purpose of God that the spiritual and cultural life of man exists and grows. In that case, how can the existence of that creative Reality be considered on the same level as that of the created? Compared to the one, the other is relatively non-existent, for the second derives its being from the former. The one is absolute and self-subsisting, the other is contingent and derived. As the Bab states, before the prophet, man should not even mention his own existence; for the very mention of it is sign that he is non-existent (33). It proves that he has not yet acquired true understanding of God's creative Purpose which, in the sphere of the spiritual and cultural life, constitutes the initial step towards progress and motion. And in the world of creation, such progress and motion are signs of existence and being.

39. THE DIFFICULTY OF SPINOZA RESIDES IN HIS FAULTY PREMISE REGARDING THE HUMAN SOUL

Spinoza's wrong assumption was that the human soul, in fact, all the world of creation, is an emanation of God's substance. And when emanation is considered as the only form of proceeding from God, then existence is bound to be considered as limited to the divine substance, which is absolute. No room is left for the relative and the contingent, for the created, as interpreted by revealed religion. Only the eternal and the uncreated would then be deemed to have existence. In other words, by identifying existence with the eternal and the absolute, Spinoza deifies the created, and overlooks the infinite range of difference that separates the Maker from what He makes: the Artisan from his object of art.

NOTES

(1) Luke 10:22.
(2) The Koran 6:103.
(3) The Persian Bayan by The Bab 3:6. (The original text has been translated into French under the title of "Le Beyan Parsan" by A. L. M. Nicolas, and published in Paris by Geuthner in 1911-14 in two volumes.)
(4) The Persian Bayan, by The Bab 4:2.

(5) Ibid. 4:6.

(6) Spinoza's Ethics, First part, Concerning God, definition II Translated by Andrew Boyle. Everyman's Library 481.

(7) Introduction to the Persian Bayan by the Bab.

(8) Ethics of Spinoza First Part. Def. III.

(9) The Persian Bayan, by the Bab 2:8.

(10) The Persian Bayan 2:15.

(11) John 8:23.

(12) Gleanings from the Writings of Baha'u'llah, tr. by Shoghi Effendi XXVII.

(13) St. John 14:6-10.

(14) Gleanings from the Writings of Baha'u'llah, tr. by Shogi Effendi LXXXIII.

(15) John 17:11.

(16) Ibid. 17:8.

(17) Ibid. 5:19.

(18) Ibid. 5:30.

(19) Koran 53:2.

(20) Prayers and Meditations of Baha'u'llah, tr. by Shoghi Effendi, p. 108.

(21) Koran 39:22.

(22) Koran 10:34.

(23) The Persian Bayan by The Bab 2:11.

(24) The Koran, 35:9.

(25) Ibid. 35:43.

(26) Ibid, 35:24.

(27) Gleanings from the Writings of Baha'u'llah, tr. by Shoghi Effendi XXXIX.

(28) The Koran 10:99.

(29) The Persian Bayan 3:6.

(30) Ibid. 3:2.

(31) Prayers and Meditations of Baha'u'llah, tr. by Shoghi Effendi LXXIX.

(32) Ibid. LVIII.

(33) The Persian Bayan, by the Bab 3:12.

CHAPTER III.

THE BASIC ETHICAL PROPOSITIONS OF SPINOZA.

We have already observed that in formulating his basic definitions upon which he built his system of Ethics, Spinoza incorporated certain primary premises and assumptions derived originally from Greek thought, but dominating Western Europe. These hypotheses, which were pagan in nature and origin, were in clear contrast to what revealed religion maintained. They were the type which springs into prominence whenever human thought loses confidence in the efficacy of revelation; that is, whenever religion experiences a recession as it did in ancient Greece; or when it rises as a mystic or philosophic movement to check the spread of a new Faith, such as we find in the appearance of Neoplatonism as spearhead of paganism against the steady progress of early Christianity.

But because Spinoza took the initial step of establishing his definitions upon conceptions such as emanation and the paramountcy of mind, their pagan tendency permeated all his thought. Especially as he chose the method of geometry, which makes its propositions logically deductive from axioms and definitions it initially presumes. The more logical, strictly deductive and absolute such mathematical reasoning is, the more clearly and distinctly the principles involved come into relief, and the conclusions reveal their peculiarity. And the more the method is pursued, and followed to its necessary conclusions, the more the contrast between these pagan principles, and revealed religion, is made striking and unavoidable. At the start, the divergeance between the doctrine of emanation and that of creation when applied to the human soul and physical

60

nature, and between the paramountcy of mind or that of spirit, might have seemed slight; but with the development of the two systems, each logically deduced from its own specific premises renders the contrast striking, and their divergence far-reaching. Especially in the field of Ethics which is the outstanding aspect of the spiritual and cultural life of the individual.

1. THE THREE WORLDS OF BEING

In answer to a question regarding the difference between mysticism and revealed religion, Abdu'l-Baha distinguishes between three worlds of being: First, the world of God as the Creator; secondly, the world of the prophets who possess two natures, the one divine, which is in substance one with God, the other human, which is in substance one with that of man. The third, is the world of created beings, the substance of which is that of an artifact, "made" by God as an artisan. This last includes both the human soul, which is spiritual, and physical nature, which is material. Such a distinction between the three worlds gives rise to the existence of two basic substances: the one divine and creator, and the other created; the one Mover, and the other moved; the one absolute and self-subsistent, the other relative, derived and contingent in being.

In contrast to such a trinitarian conception, which establishes two forms of proceeding from God—one as emanation, which is peculiar to the divine nature revealed in the prophets, and the other created and characteristic of the human soul and of physical being—Spinoza, we observed, maintains the existence of only one form of proceeding, namely emanation, which establishes substantial oneness between God and the world of nature, including the human soul. In other words, he tries to eliminate completely any distinction between the divine nature of the prophets and the human soul, and thereby obviate the need for an intermediary world of the prophets which operates as a mirror reflecting divine light to mankind. Thus, while revealed religion maintains a trinity of the world of being and a plurality of substance Spinoza upholds a monistic conception, both of reality and being, and of substance. And upon this basic conception he tries to establish the foundations of his Ethics. To him there is only one substance which is both natural and divine. All things, whether physical and material, or intellectual and spiritual, are merely modes of that one substance. To establish that monism securely as a primary premise, he starts by attacking the principle of creation, upheld by revealed religion, which maintains the plurality of substance; on the ground that all things are but modifications of that one Being which is God, or nature; though he admits that "a substance is prior in its nature to its modifications"(Prop. 1): that is, that God should be considered as prior to His "modes," found as individual objects of nature; just as a sea is prior to the waves that surge in it.

2. CONTRAST BETWEEN UNITY OF SUBSTANCE, AND UNITY OF CREATIVE PURPOSE

Revealed religion considers the unity of the universe, based upon the unity of a transcendent creative purpose which is God's. We observe that clearly in the Bayan which says that, the divine Essence, being an absolutely transcendent reality, unknowable to man, generates the Primal Purpose; and this latter, in turn, creates all other being. The Bab identifies this reality with the Primal Point which sets the limits and definitions of things and also with the "Word" or "Wisdom" which is the source of all knowledge and understanding. He further identifies all these realities with the divine nature revealed in the prophets. In other words, we might consider them all as "modes" of that supreme Substance or God. This primal Purpose, which the Bab regards as the supreme creative Force in the universe, is the uniting reality that sets all things in motion and directs their course. That Primal Purpose not only unites this pluralistic universe into a single organic harmonious whole but also makes physical nature, the individual human soul, society and its history, the spiritual and cultural life of man, all, dynamic, constantly moving, integrating and reintegrating into higher forms of existence. This Primal Purpose moves and vitalizes all things, and directs their course towards a determined goal, while remaining itself transcendent to nature and its physical and intellectual life and being. In contrast to this dynamic, and purposeful, conception presented by the Bab, we have that of Spinoza, which tries to establish the unity of the universe, upon the unity of its primary substance. Hence, he eliminates the emphasis of religion upon constant reintegration of "improvement," stressed by the doctrine of creation. To establish his pantheism, however, Spinoza had to start by showing that, the plurality of substantial being, held by revealed religion, is untenable.

3. THE PRINCIPLE THAT ONLY LIKE CAN KNOW ITS LIKE

Another favorite principle of ancient Greek thought was that only a "like can know its like"; that is, that unity of substance alone can be the basis of thought and understanding. If two substances are unlike, they cannot understand each other. We find that principle maintained by Spinoza as a fundamental axiom of his thought; for he says: "Things which have nothing in common reciprocally cannot be comprehended reciprocally through each other, or, the conception of the one does not involve the conception of the other"(Axiom 5). Upon this axiom Spinoza bases his second and third propositions which run as follows: "Two substances, having different attributes, have nothing in common between them." "Of two things having nothing in common between them, one cannot be the cause of the other." His proof for this proposition is that "if they have nothing in common reciprocally, therefore they cannot be known through each other, and therefore one cannot be the cause of the other." In other words, because in conformity with a pluralistic conception of being, such as the doctrine of creation maintains, there is no unity of substance, and no unity of form or attribute, between the Creator and the created; because of this, the one cannot be known through the other; and hence, the one cannot be considered as the cause of the other. In short, both the epistemological and the ontological approach to being is considered by Spinoza to be based upon unity of substance. Only when two realities are substantially and formally "like," Spinoza maintains, can they know each other.

4. THOUGH SUBSTANTIALLY, AND FORMALLY, AND HENCE ONTOLOGICALLY THE CREATOR IS UNLIKE THE CREATED, HE KNOWS IT

In knowledge, the crucial point is not whether the conception of the one substance contains the conception of the other, as Spinoza holds it to be. This requirement of the principle of knowledge is derived from a distorted approach of an "observer" to an objective reality. Besides the fact that this requirement of the principle of knowledge, held by Spinoza, is fully satisfied in the doctrine of creation—for the conception of Creator necessarily implies the conception of the created—yet, that is not the crucial point. What is crucial, and of paramount significance, in establishing the ultimate criterion of knowledge and understanding is whether it is the point of view of the "creator" of the object. Because, whereas the relation between the "observer" and the observed, is not necessary, that between the Creator and the created, is. The Mover is the efficient Cause of the being of the moved. Therefore, the crucial, and essential, point is that the one substance should be acting as the efficient Cause of the nature and being of the other. The creator visualizes a certain form, then chooses a certain substance as matter, molds that form into its fabric as pattern, and thereby generates a new individual substantial entity. The form visualized, the material chosen, and the full process of incorporating the one into the other, all are the direct result of the conscious will and purpose of the creator. And this constitutes the ground of his knowledge and understanding. But to the creator, that idea, or form, does not constitute the full reality and existence of the object. It was Greek rationalism, which took the point of view of the "observer," that identified the idea, or form, with the substance of a thing. On that rationalistic ground substance applied first and foremost to the idea or form; and possessed priority of being. Substance is thus made to apply to the form, idea, and considered existent in the mind of God as an abiding reality. To revealed religion, however, the substance of a thing is in its individual existence, which results from, and is subsequent to, its creation or regeneration. The idea, or pattern, of that individual resides in the divine mind only as an inchoate being; just as a formula of a chemical composition originates in the mind of a chemist as an abstraction, or inchoate idea: as a thing to be made objective and to acquire substantial reality after a process of synthesis. It is after that integration and synthesis that it becomes existent.

5. THE CREATOR AND THE CREATED HAVE NO ATTRIBUTE IN COMMON, YET THE ONE IS THE EFFICIENT CAUSE OF THE OTHER

Because the idea, or pattern, originates in the mind of the Creator and then proceeds from him through a conscious and intelligent progress to its final actualization, it constitutes not only a direct object of knowledge and understanding, but its very product. And this knowledge comprises the idea, the nature of the material employed, and the substance of individual object created. This initial knowledge of all the factors employed, and the subsequent conscious and intelligent actualization of it in an individual being, renders the knowledge of the Creator, in regard to

64

the object created, certain and absolute. On the other hand, because the observer can possess no such initial knowledge of these factors, because they are not the product of its intelligent purpose, and has not actively pursued, or participated, in that creative act, he can lay no claim to such knowledge.

"Every praise which any tongue or pen can recount," says Baha'u'l-lah, "every imagination which any heart can devise, is debarred from the station which Thy most exalted Pen hath ordained, how much more must it fall short of the heights which Thou has Thyself immensely above the conception and the description of any creature. For the attempt of the evanescent to conceive the signs of the Uncreated is as the stirring of the drop before the tumult of Thy billowing oceans. Nay, forbid it, O my God, that I should thus venture to describe Thee, for every similitude and comparison must pertain to what is essentially created by Thee. How can then such similitude and comparison ever befit Thee, or reach up unto Thy self?"(1)

In other words, should the Creator be not positively and accurately known through, and by, the created, on the ground that Spinoza states, namely, "that the conception of the one does not involve the conception of the other"; this would not prove that the one is not the cause of the other, as he proceeds to conclude. The fact that the conception of "thought," and of "body," as created realities, does not give us an adequate conception of God, is no ground for maintaining that the latter is not the efficient Cause of the former. In fact, because this latter is the Creator, He absolutely transcends any conception the former may make of Him. In short, the Creator and the created "have nothing in common reciprocally," and yet the former has absolute knowledge of the other.

6. THIS FIFTH AXIOM APPLIES BETWEEN GOD AND HIS PROPHETS

This axiom of Spinoza applies only when the proceeding from God is in the nature of emanation. Hence, it applies only to the divine nature revealed in the prophets, in its relation with God. Unity of conception, or unity of the attributes conceived, which Spinoza considers axiomatic in his reasoning, applies to the doctrine of emanation. For, under that condition alone, substantial unity is maintained, and the attributes of perfection we state for God, as efficient Cause, are considered the attributes of perfection we find revealed in the prophets, as the formal

Cause of man's spiritual and cultural life. The axiom does not apply to proceeding through creation, when God is considered the "maker," and man the "made" or formed.

7. DIFFERENCE OF ATTRIBUTES DENOTES DIFFERENCE OF SUBSTANCE

In proposition III, Spinoza attempted to show that, "two things have nothing in common between them, one cannot be the cause of the other." In proposition IV he tries to prove that, two or more things which differ either in attribute or in mode, are different. "Two or three distinct things are distinguished one from the other either by the difference of the attributes of the substances or by the difference of their modifications" (Prop. 4). In other words, in distinguishing between objects, Spinoza considers difference of attributes, and difference of modes, on the same level as ground for differentiation.

Thus, under the doctrine of emanation, when unity of substance is maintained, the difference of attributes, and difference of modes, are made coextensive and identical. But under the doctrine of creation, when no such unity of substance between the creator and the created is asserted, the difference of attributes cannot be identified with difference of modes and made coextensive. Each possesses its own sphere of operation, depending on whether the proceeding from God is through emanation or through creation.

We have already observed that, under the doctrine of creation, while difference of attributes proves difference of substance, difference of modes implies its unity. If attributes are properties and characteristics, actions and reactions, that a substance habitually reveals, then basic difference between attributes proves difference of substance, as their source and mainstay. For the same reality, or substance, cannot be deemed to possess contrary forms of action and reaction, and contain contradictory elements within its nature. It is otherwise in the case of modes. To the very extent that difference of attributes denotes difference of substance difference of modes implies unity of the underlying substances. The substance of vapour, ice, and the sea with its surging waves—similarly the light which proceeds from the sun, and the one reflected by the mirror—the substance of each group is the same, though their modes differ. For members of that group can be reduced one into the other. On the other hand, if we are presented with two realities revealing basically different attributes, we infer that their underlying substance is different. For example, if we take the divine reality in the prophets the function of which is to reveal God's attributes of perfection to mankind; and on the other, the human soul, the peculiarity of which is to receive those attributes, and gradually acquire them and make them its own; if we find this fundamental difference between these two realities, then we conclude that the underlying substance of the one is different from that of the other. That the nature of the one is to move; that of the other is to be moved.

To speak, therefore, of "body" and "thought," or of physical being and the human soul, as "attributes" of the same substance of God or to maintain that the human soul and the Spirit of Christ, which constitutes the divine nature revealed in the prophets, are in substance one and the same is, according to the doctrine of creation, utterly incorrect. For their basic functions and characteristics are different and contrary. The one creates and regenerates, the other is created and regenerated by it. Similarly, compared to physical nature, the human soul is creative and mover; while the latter is as clay moved, and constantly remolded, at the hands of man; and used by him as instrument in his, albeit limited, sphere of creative activity. As the one is creative and the other passive they are substantially different. This passivity, on the one hand, and activity, on the other, proves that they are substantially different: that the one is not merely a "mode" of the other, with the two "modes" of a higher reality.

8. DIFFERENT SUBSTANCES CANNOT POSSESS THE SAME ATTRIBUTES

Spinoza, we observed, tries to eliminate the distinction between difference of mode, and that of attributes, to maintain the unity of substance, fundamental for his pantheism. Therefore, he takes the converse of his previous proposition, and says: "In the nature of things, two or more substances may not be granted having the same nature or attributes." (Prop. V) Spinoza takes up the case when difference of attributes prevails and might be considered as the ground of difference of substance because this is peculiar to the principle of creation, held by revealed religion, which he tries to combat. Cases of difference of modes, do not impair the doctrine of emanation, and its unity of substance. "Since substance is prior in its nature to its modifications," he says, "therefore, let the modifications be laid aside and let the substance itself be considered in itself, that is truly considered, and it could not then be distinguished from another. . . ." (Proof of Prop. 5) It is the doctrine of creation and its pluralism which he tries to assail. Therefore, he says, "One substance cannot be produced by another" (Prop. VI). His proof for this proposition is that, "In the nature of things two substances cannot be granted with the same attribute (prev. Prop), that is (Prop. 2) which have anything in common, and accordingly (Prop. 3) one of them cannot be the cause of the other or one cannot be produced by the other."

But as we have already observed, neither Prop. 2, nor Prop. 3, is applicable to cases proceeding from God, in the form of creation. According to the doctrine of emanation, which constitutes the basic hypothetical premise of Spinoza's thought, God is an intelligible reality, in the nature of Mind. So is "thought," or the human soul, and "body," that is, physical nature, in so far as its substance is formal. Being all formal, intelligible, and in the nature of "thought," he would argue they possess the same attributes and hence, they are substantially the same. Therefore, there can be no plurality, one being considered the cause of the other such as revealed religion maintains. The contrary hypothesis, which revealed religion maintains, is that God is not in the nature of "mind," that He transcends understanding, and therefore, is not intelligible, and cannot possibly have anything in common with the human soul, or with physical nature, which are merely His handiwork. Mind is a psychological function of the human soul, to which it transcends. The latter is the mover, and the former instrumental and the moved. Hence, there are no common attributes between God and the human soul, or between the latter and physical being. In other words, there is basic difference of attributes between them; therefore, their substance is different. In short, the proof of Spinoza would stand only if his basic hypothetical premises are true, which, according to revealed religion, they are not. His proof would stand only if the human soul, and physical nature, would have proceeded from God, as emanation and not as creation: not as individual realities which, as such, were integrated into higher types of being.

9. THE INDIVIDUAL IS SUBJECT AND NEVER PREDICATE, AND HENCE, IS SUBSTANTIAL

Another proof, which Spinoza advances to establish that, "one substance cannot be produced by another," is that, "this can be more easily shown by the method of proving the contrary to be absurd. For if a substance can be produced from anything else, the knowledge of it would depend on the knowledge of its cause (Ax. 4), and consequently, (Def. 5) it would not be substance.''

Spinoza's definition of substance, as we have already observed, is rationalistic and formal while ontologically substance is individual. It is the individual that acts and reacts to its environment and, as such, reveals properties and attributes, or can be made to assume a higher form, and thereby, rise to a higher state of being, with a new individuality and a higher substantial reality. The principle of self-subsistence, which Spinoza's definition maintains as basis of substantiality, applies, as we have already observed, only to the absolute unmoved Mover, or God. That is absolutely true. But individual created objects also can act and react to their environment, be substrata of qualities, properties and attributes. All created objects, in the hands of a competent creator, are made to acquire a higher form, and rise to a higher level of being and individuality and thereby reveal higher attributes and a stage of substantial being. And because these individual entities can so act as the substrata of action and reaction, they can be viewed as subject of predicates. Does not an object of art act as substratum to qualities we may impress on it; and does that not make it the subject of predicates?

Having acquired higher, and therefore, different attributes, objects of art become substantially different and higher, with a new acquired reality. For different attributes, according to Spinoza himself, imply different substantiality. As created individual objects, and hence moved, they will not be self-subsistent and absolute in being; their substantiality will be contingent, and derived from a higher source; but nevertheless they will be substantial. An object of art, as an individual created entity, is substantial, and can act as substratum to any form or attribute the artist may choose to impress upon it; it can therefore act as subject to predicates, which the artist desires; but still, it depends upon the artist for its substantiality and being. If we deny substantiality to the object of art, we deny creative power to the artist as well. Therefore, it is substantial though created and contingent; and the idea, or form, it represents, has had its origin in the creative genius of its ''maker,'' and ''improver.''

Spinoza could not admit such a created substance, and remain true to his premise that emanation is the only form of proceeding from God, that the individual human soul, and the individual physical objects in nature, are mere "modes," different from the divine substance, not in attributes, but only in modality. He could not admit the unity of substance of qualitatively different created objects and not impair his monism. And if he had admitted different substantiality to the human soul, from that of God, and hence, different attributes, he would be under the obligation to discover an intermediate reality, which possessed those attributes, and which would act as the direct source of the ethical life and thus establish that which revealed religion maintains.

10. DOES ESSENCE NECESSARILY INVOLVE EXISTENCE?

"Existence," says Spinoza, "appertains to the nature of substance" (Prop. VII). Its proof is that "a substance cannot be produced from anything else (Prov. Prop): it will therefore be its own cause, that is (Def. 1), its essence necessarily involved existence, or existence appertains to the nature of it." We have already observed that under the rationalistic system of thought, which attributes priority of substance and reality to the universal idea or form, instead of to the particular and individual, existence appertains equally to the essence and to the substance. And that on the ground that definition, nature, substance, essence, existence, all are attributed primarily to the conceptual reality, to the idea or form, which is the supremely intelligible and rational. Under such circumstances, not only "existence appertains to the nature of substance" (Prop. 7), but also "its essence necessarily involves existence"(Proof). In other words, substance is identified with essence, and both considered as necessarily existent.

Substance denotes the "stuff" of which a reality is constituted; such as when Jesus said "God is a spirit," to distinguish His nature from "mind" or the way physical objects were held by philosophy and the paganism of the age. Essence denotes the qualities and characteristics that reality possesses and reveals such as when we attribute to Him existence and other attributes of perfection. To identify these two, namely, substance and essence, with existence in God, it is generally held that the very conception of the one implies the conception of the other. Perfection necessitates existence for the non-existent cannot be deemed perfect. And if it has existence, it should be considered as able to act as substratum for those attributes of perfection. But this is a purely rationalistic and conceptual approach to the subject and tends to make human understanding the criterion of its truth, which is wrong. But there is an ontological approach to the subject, which falls in line with our reasoning, and is more self-explanatory; namely, when we differentiate between the field of emanation and that of creation.

11. IN GOD ALONE, HENCE ACCORDING TO THE DOCTRINE OF EMANATION, ESSENCE IMPLIES SUBSTANCE AND EXISTENCE

The Bab says that, for the names of God, that is, for His attributes of perfection, there is no limit and number (2). If the essence of God is His characteristics, or attributes of perfection, then these do imply their necessary existence. For these perfections could not have existed if they were not actually revealed through the divine nature of the prophets. The mere fact of their revelation as essence of God is proof that they possess existence, and constitute aspects of the divine substance. If the light, which illuminates human understanding, comes as a reflection in a mirror, then that very reflection implies that it has a higher source with full substantial reality and existence emitting that light. When two entities have common substance, and hence, common essence and attributes, unity of substance, essence and existence in the one imply unity of substance, essence and existence in the other. In other words, the same necessary connection that exists between the substance and essence in the one exists between the substance and essence of the other: for this is what the doctrine of emanation is taken to premise. When we speak of God's Wisdom, Goodness, Justice, Beauty, Dominion, Sovereignty, as the essense of His substance, it is because these constitute the expression of the divine nature revealed in His prophets. The necessary connection in the latter implies necessary connection in the former. They are fully actual in the prophets, hence, we say they are fully actual in God.

The case is otherwise in the field of creation; where there is neither unity of substance, nor unity of attributes between the creator and the created; where perfections are merely to be acquired. Here the conception of a quality, and attribute, does not necessitate its being in actuality. It merely implies the possibility of its acquisition. In the divine nature revealed in the prophets attributes of perfection are "hidden" (3) and potential; the occasion will render them manifest and actual. The human soul has merely the capacity of acquiring them in its process of evolution. "Potentiality" implies existence, "capacity" does not. It merely implies

71

the possibility of acquiring those attributes. It implies that they are not initially present and existing, that they will become so after a process of "improvement" and a corresponding lapse of time.

Is there an identity between the pattern, definition or essence and the particular object after the process of its creation into a substantial being? An essence, if identified with form, in the mind of the creator, or maker, has a conceptual, universal, abstract and inchoate reality while the object, once created, is objective, concrete, and individual. There is marked difference between the Kingdom of God visualized as an abstract concept, the different aspects of which Jesus tried to explain in his parables, and the concrete, objective and positive one, foretold to come "on earth." The one was universal and ideal, the other particular: a political and social state of society, expected to be established in time, as the realization of the Lord's prayer. The one was conceptual; the other substantial and existent.

Essence is thus universal, like all definitions and mathematical formula. The existence is particular and substantial. The first is merely the inchoate pattern of the second. The two cannot be confused and identified in this world of creation. In the rationalistic system of thought, and under the doctrine of emanation, essence, substance and existence can imply one another: not so in revealed religion, with its principle of the creation of the human soul, and the world of physical nature.

12. CAN EXISTENCE, WHICH IS AN ATTRIBUTE, PREDICATE A SUBSTANCE ADMITTED TO BE TRANSCENDENT?

"Existence," says Spinoza, "appertains to the nature of substance" (Prop. VII). We have considered this proposition ontologically, in the light of both the doctrines of emanation and of creation, respectively; but there is an epistemological aspect to it as well. Greek thought maintained that man is the measure of all things. It could not, therefore, maintain that God transcends human understanding and thought without impairing that supreme measure. For if God, Who is the supreme Being, is unknowable, and beyond the grasp of human understanding, then man can not be regarded as the "measure" of all things, both of their nature and existence. Unless we are bold enough to assert that having failed to satisfy that supreme criterion of His existence and nature, God is non-existent, and constitutes a mere product of human imagining. To avoid such an atheistic alternative, Rationalism had to maintain that God is the supreme object of understanding, and that the idea of Him, being clear and distinct, is true. In other words, Rationalism could not consider God as the object of intellection, unless it took for granted that His nature constituted factual objects of human understanding. Spinoza was heir to that rationalistic premise, and therefore, had to be true to its conclusions.

Being, or existence, is a predicate we assign to God when we say that He "is." If it is a predicate, it constitutes an attribute or quality we give Him. But His absolute transcendence to human thought and understanding precludes such assumption. Hence, strictly speaking, even existence cannot be attributed to God: even His existence is made object of human knowledge only through the fact of His revelation. As Baha'u'llah says, to admit frankly our inability to fathom the mystery of God's nature and essence is "the acme of human understanding, and maketh the culmination of man's development"(4). "Far, far from Thy glory be what mortal man affirm of Thee, or attribute unto Thee, or the praise with which he can glorify Thee!"(2)

In the Bayan, the Bab says that God has made His essence the very being of His Primal Purpose (6). In other words, in the Primal Purpose divine substance, being and essence are considered united and identified. And they ought to be, according to our previous reasoning, if the former is an emanation of the latter. Furthermore, the Primal Purpose is the divine nature revealed in the prophets (7). Hence, just as existence "appertains to the nature of substance" in God's being, so it is in the divine nature revealed in the prophets. With these primary premises we come to the conclusion that substance, essence, or divine perfections, are existent absolutely and epistemologically ascertained, not in a transcendent God which is far beyond human grasp and understanding, but in an entity which had been manifested, or revealed by Him, to become object of human knowledge and understanding.

Furthermore, as this supreme object of human understanding is a revelation from God, man is not considered the measure of its efficacy and truth. Its knowledge is in God, as the Bab says, and through Himself it is revealed in His creature, because He has created him (8). In other words, God possesses that knowledge, not on the ground that man has discovered it, setting as observer and imagining, but because He was conscious of his nature and being while creating it. The truth that the divine nature revealed in the prophets combines necessary substance and existence and attributes of perfection in their full actual form is because it is in substance divine and Creator of all things other than Him. It is because its Wisdom is God's. Human intellect operates only to verify that truth, amplify it, and discover its applications. In other words, the principle of the identity or necessary mutual implication of existence and substance in the divine nature is through the emanation of the divine nature revealed in the prophets; whereby it becomes an empirical and historical fact, if empiricism be interpreted as verification of a truth already given, put to the test of experience. And if we go further with the Bab, and state that the image we observe in the mirror is not in the mirror itself, but in the reality beyond which it reflects (9), then we come to the conclusion that the substance of God, together with His essence are existent in Him, as transcendent reality.

13. EQUIVOCATION OF THE TERM INFINITY

"All substance," says Spinoza, "is necessarily infinite" (Prop. VIII). Let us now consider more specifically the attribute infinity, which Spinoza predicates to both God and nature. God is a mover; nature is moved; hence, motion implies a process, a constant becoming. What we can rightly assert of this process, is that it never started, and that it will never end: that an eternal Mover necessarily implies an eternal process of motion, and an infinite reality which is moved. Both the Mover and the moved are eternal in reality, and in that sense, infinite. But the eternity and infinity of the one is essentially different from the eternity and infinity of the other. The eternity and infinity of the one is as Mover; the eternity and infinity of the other is in being moved. The one is free and creative; the other is guided and compelled in its course. But though the infinity of the two is essentially and basically different in nature, they are complementary, and necessitate one another. The one is the field of man's possible evolution; the other is the power which stimulates and guides that growth. Infinity or unending process of motion, in acquiring perfection, is essentially different from an infinity of actuality as regards the possession of those perfections. The one is subject to time, and the categories of understanding; the other is far beyond time and human thought and grasp. In fact we cannot imagine what infinity beyond the process of becoming is: what a timeless, spaceless, unchanging infinity is. It constitutes one of the predicates which we cannot with full justification attribute to an absolutely transcendent God.

Pagan thought, which identified God with the universe, including the human soul, and physical being, could talk of infinity in one specific sense, that is, as temporal duration, and spacial limitlessness: hence, the conception of infinity of God, and infinity of nature could be, considered together, put in apposition, and made mutually exclusive. But in revealed religion, with its doctrine of creation, the infinity attributed to God as Creator and the infinity predicated of creation, far from contradicting each other, complement and necessitate one another. It is the pagan conception of the universe, which Spinoza adopted, and with which he got involved, that led him to the predicaments arising from its logical implications. Put on the same level of space, and the same process of time, they could limit each other. But when causally related through the process of creation, they were not. Infinity of cause necessitates infinity of effect.

14. DISTINCTION BETWEEN APPEARANCE AND REALITY IS MORE APPLICABLE TO THE PRINCIPLE OF EMANATION

In the first note appended to Proposition VIII, Spinoza makes his attack on the doctrine of creation more specific. He says: "To call anything finite is, in reality, a denial in part, and to call it infinite is the absolute assertion of the existence of its nature, it follows, therefore, (from Prop. VII) that all substance must be infinite." In other words, that besides substance, which is absolutely existent, and its modes; there can be no substance whose existence is contingent, in the sense, of being derived from a higher reality, in an act of creation and finite.

"Denial in part," if taken as a principle, in conjunction with the modality of "body" and "thought," boils down to the distinction usually made between "appearance" and "reality." For the former is considered as a mere "sign," or "expression," of the latter, which is considered "hidden" from human empirical experience. Addressing the divine nature revealed in the prophets, that is, the Primal Purpose which is manifest in them all, the Bab says: "You are the appearance" (10): in other words, the revelation of God's attributes of perfection, when contrasted with the absolute divine substance and reality. Inasmuch as the divine nature revealed in the prophets, is one in substance with God, and constitutes a mere reflection of His attributes; it is an "appearance." Considered otherwise, elements of dualism will appear in the divine nature. As the substance of that reflected reality is not in the human nature of the prophets acting as a mirror but in the transcendent God, the divine nature in them can be termed mere "appearance," which is what Spinoza considers "denial in part." In fact, as the Bab remarks, the virtue of a mirror is in that it is selfless (11). The fullness of its reflection is in direct proportion to its self-denial, to the fact that it has no inherent characteristics which would distort the effulgent light of God. If any reality, acting as a mirror, and reflecting the light of God, directs its attention to its own inherent characteristics as mirror, says the Bab, it immediately ceases to reflect that light faithfully and adequately. In other words, that entity constitutes as much of an appearance as the rays of light reflected in the mirror and its virtue is in being a mere reflection, a faithful "appearance" of a transcendent reality. This principle is imbedded in the doctrine of emanation, when the reality emanated is considered in substance one with God and differentiated only as a "mode," or an "outflowing," or "reflection," of it.

But when the principle of "appearance," or "denial in part," is applied to the world of creation, the result is otherwise. Surely, a created reality cannot be compared in substance and being to its creator. That subject has already been dealt with. But the reality of the creative Power, of the Primal Purpose, is in direct proportion to the reality of the object created. It is not only the infinity of the creative reality, which determines the infinity of the creative Power, and Purpose but also the measure of the reality created. The fuller and higher the reality of the object created the more dominating and effective the creative Power and Purpose proves to be. It is only the mystics, and advocates of the doctrine of emanation as the universal form of proceeding from God, who stress the non-reality of the world of nature and of the individuality of the human soul. To the prophets these are real, even though they are contingent, created, and sustained by God as their Creator. And their reality is progressive, depending upon their stage of development, the extent they have been reborn into a higher form of life. The self-denial demanded from the human soul, is not substantial, but of will and purpose. We are asked to be selfless, and submit our will to God's, not to minimise our individual substantial reality but to enhance it, to make it better molded by the creative Purpose, to better acquire attributes of perfection, and develop a personality distinctly its own.

15. TO BE FINITE DOES NOT NECESSARILY MEAN TO BE "IN PART DENIED"

Furthermore, as already observed, to say with revealed religion that nature is "finite" does not mean that it is "in part denied." It merely means that the efficient Cause of its being is attributed to another than itself, that is, to a reality that transcends it. In fact, revealed religion maintains that nature is indefinitely extended in time and in space, that it has had no beginning, and can have no end. But that does not obviate the fact that, within nature individual substances are being constantly integrated, from a lower state of being, to a higher one. Referring to God, the Bab repeatedly assigns to Him creation, sustenance, causing death and imparting life. God does not only bring into being, He also sustains the individuals composing this universe. Sustenance, and imparting new form and life, counteract the principle of death and disintegration and maintain the balance, and "improvement" which prevail in the universe.

Nature is a universal term: an intellectual abstraction. What is substantial, and real, is the individual objects composing it. These are the objects to which creation, sustenance, death and imparting new life apply. And these objects are limited and finite. These individuals are substantial because they move, act and react; and also because they are always subject and never predicate. The existence of these individual objects, including the individual human soul, cannot be considered as "in part denied"; for they are not mere "appearances." The reality of the individual human soul, which in the supreme reality in the world of creation, is not a mere "seeming," as mystics with their doctrine of universal emanation, and unity of substance, would have it said. It is fully real and substantial, otherwise God's creation, sustenance, inflicting death, and imparting new life, would lose its significance, and Primary Purpose.

What revealed religion maintains is that integration, which it terms creation, cannot be due to a force, or efficient Cause, "hidden" and immanent in these individual substances nor in nature as an abstract reality; for if it were immanent in them, death or disintegration would not exist to be balanced by imparting life and being. That universal law and order would cease to operate. Elements composing a compound would not separate if the uniting and integrating power and agency were inherent in the elements and operating. The fact of disintegration, its very possibility, implies the non-existence of that integrating force, not that it is merely hidden in that sphere of operation. The mere fact that culture can fall back to the level of nature, and deteriorate spiritually, is sufficient proof that the integrating and creative force, derived from the prophets, is not operative. Otherwise there could be no cultural disintegration. In other words, the fact of disintegration, the possibility of spiritual death, proves that integration is due to a transcendent force, or efficient Cause, which only periodically is revealed in the world. This absolute dependence of individual substantial objects, upon an efficient, transcendent, integrating Force, or Primary Purpose, is the type of finiteness we attribute to the human soul and other objects in nature; and that does not imply a "denial in part," or mere "appearance" of reality. The physical elements in the object have to obtain an optimum condition, but also a transcendent force has to operate to provide the new form to existing matter.

16. SUBSTANCE AS SELF-SUBSISTING

In his second note to Proposition VIII, Spinoza reverts back to the distinction made between substance and its modifications. He defines substance as that "which is in itself, and through itself is conceived" and considers modification as "that which is in something else, and whose conception is formed from the conception of whatever it is in." Thus, whereas a "substance" is considered as self-subsisting both ontologically and epistemologically, a "mode" is regarded as self-subsisting neither ontologically nor epistemologically. It exists, and is known, through a reality other than itself, individually. And because these "modes" are known through other than themselves, individually, "we may have true ideas of modifications which do not exist." In other words, they may be likened to conceptions for which there is no corresponding thing in itself. These modifications therefore may be known through their essences, or characteristics, which exist in the mind, or through the substance of which they are modifications. Spinoza then proceeds to say that because the essence of a substance is that it should exist in itself, and be known only by itself, we cannot possess a clear and distinct idea of it except if we regard it as existent. For both existence and essence reside in the substance, where they are conjoined and identified. Under such circumstances the idea, or essence, of a substance includes its existence. And to maintain that a substance is created, that is, has its cause in other than itself, amounts to saying "that a false idea might be made true."

17. THE ONTOLOGICAL ASPECT OF SPINOZA'S DEFINITION OF SUBSTANCE

The definition Spinoza gives here of "substance" has two aspects: first, the ontological, which is expressed by the term "is in itself"; and secondly, the epistemological, implied in the expression "conceived" through itself. Let us consider each aspect separately. We have already observed that the reason why an entity is substantial is that it acts and reacts as a unit in a manner peculiar to itself, and therefore has functions and attributes all its own. These functions and attributes distinguish it from other individual substances, because difference of attributes admittedly implies difference of substance. But this does not avoid the possibility of that substance to be created, and of having its efficient cause in other than itself. In fact, there is no possible justification for identifying the substance of the Creator and the created when they act and react differently, and hence their attributes are different, when their functions stand in contrast one with the other. A created object, once created, acts and reacts in a manner all its own and hence fulfils functions peculiar to itself. To revert to the Bab's example of a mirror, the actual glass has attributes and functions all its own, totally different from the rays of light or image reflected in it. Each has its own peculiar function. Hence they cannot be identified. The one cannot be considered a "mode" of the other for they do not possess unity of attribute and function. In short, ontologically an entity is substantial whether or not it is a Creator or created, whether its efficient cause is in itself, or in other than itself. It is substantial because it acts and reacts as a unit, and possesses functions all its own. Its substantiality is not determined by whether it is self-subsisting or contingent, whether it is moved or constitutes the Mover. In the world of creation every object has its efficient Cause in a reality other and higher than itself, but once "made" it has functions and attributes all its own and on that ground possesses substantial existence.

18. THE EPISTEMOLOGICAL ASPECT OF SPINOZA'S DEFINITION OF SUBSTANCE

Let us now consider the epistemological aspect of Spinoza's definition of substance. All his very close reasoning rests upon the rationalistic premise that substance, especially ultimate substance, which is God's, constitutes the highest object of knowledge and understanding. We have already observed that essence is the definition of a reality, while substance is its existent element. The first is an object of understanding; the second constitutes the ground of its being. We approach the first epistemologically, the second ontologically. The ontological element of a "mode" is in the substance of which it is a "mode"; just as the image we observe in the mirror, as the Bab says, resides in the reality reflected, not in the glass. On the other hand, the ontological element of a "created thing" is in the created thing itself, that is, in the mirror or glass. In this latter field there is no possibility of essence, definition or knowledge which an observer can attain. For substance by its very nature eludes him. Substance is the product of creative activity which is an ontological process and is known solely to the creator, by whom it was molded into being. For an observer who does not participate in the creative activity and is not ontologically involved, the only field for knowledge and understanding is that of "mode," "appearance," or "phenomenon." Mode alone can be the object of "clear and distinct" idea or understanding to an observer. The aspect we apprehend, either of nature or of God, can be only their "mode," "appearance" or phenomena of their revelation, not their substance itself. As Baha'u'llah says, we cannot know the substance of a stone. Then how can we claim to know the substance of the human soul, or of God? Man's understanding is limited to the field of attributes or "modes" revealed by that substance. It can never penetrate further into the realm of their underlying substance. That substance may be that of the "Mover" or of the "moved," of the Creator or of the created. Between a "mode" and its corresponding substance there is unity of attributes; between different substances there can be none. In other words, substance cannot be conceived through itself, as Spinoza maintains, for the simple reason that substance cannot be the object of understanding. On the other hand, "mode" need not be conceived through the substance in which it is, because it is itself the direct object of understanding.

19. "MODES" CONSTITUTE THE DIRECT OBJECTS OF UNDERSTANDING

Thus, if we set aside the rationalistic principle that substance is knowable, that it constitutes the most "distinct and clear" idea, and uphold instead the doctrine of revealed religion, namely, that only the "modes" of being, their emanation or appearances are object of understanding; further, if we add to this belief the principle already stressed, namely that unity of attributes implies unity of substance and difference of attributes difference of substance; if we accept these two notions, we come to the conclusion that physical substances, and the human soul, can be known only through the "modes" or "appearances," which reveal its attributes. Natural phenomena, as "modes" of natural substance, reveal the actions and reactions, that is, attributes and properties of natural substances; and the divine nature, reflected in the prophets, acting as "mode" of the divine Substance, reveals the creative power, and attributes of perfection of God.

If unity of attributes is what renders a certain entity, a "mode" of a certain substance; then phenomena in nature become "modes" of God's substance only if He is regarded a naturalistic God and identified with the Universe or the forces and laws that permeate it. If, on the other hand, God is considered the Creator and "maker" of all realities other than Himself, then His attributes of perfection transcend the forces of nature and the physical universe and can be known only through entities that bear unity of attributes with Him: entities which as "modes" of His being reveal those attributes. And these have been, not objects of nature, or the human soul, but the prophets of God that have appeared at regular intervals down the ages.

"These sanctified mirrors," says Baha'u'llah, "these Day Springs of ancient glory, are, one and all, the Exponents on earth of Him Who is the central Orb of the universe, its Essence and ultimate Purpose. From Him proceed their knowledge and power; from Him is derived their sovereignty. The beauty of their countenance is but a reflection of His image, and their revelation a sign of His deathless glory. They are the Treasuries of Divine knowledge, and the Repositories of celestial wisdom. Through them is transmitted a grace that is infinite, and by them is revealed the Light that can never fade. . . . These Tabernacles of Holiness, these Primal Mirrors which reflect the light of unfading glory, are but expressions of Him Who is the Invisible of the Invisibles. By the revelation of these Gems of Divine virtue all the names and attributes of God, such as knowledge and power, sovereignty and dominion, mercy and wisdom, glory, bounty, and grace, are made manifest.

"These attributes of God are not, and have never been, vouchsafed specially unto certain prophets, and withheld from others. Nay, all the Prophets of God, His well-favoured, His holy and chosen Messengers are, without exception, the bearers of His names, and the embodiment of His attributes. They only differ in the intensity of their revelation, and the comparative potency of their light. Even as He hath revealed: 'Some of the Apostles We have caused to excel others.' " (12).

20. NECESSARY ELEMENTS OF A DEFINITION

After defining substance as that which exists in itself and attempting to prove that essence and substance are necessarily identified in absolute reality, Spinoza concludes that "there cannot be two substances of the same nature." In this connection, he lays down the necessary elements of an adequate definition which he enumerates as (a) the nature of that thing, (b) as an individual definite entity, (c) together with the cause of its existence as such. He further argues that there can be two possible causes operating, namely, a cause immanent in the nature of that object or one that transcends it.

Now, if definition is of a definite entity, Spinoza argues, it must be of a particular; and if it has to state the efficient cause of the being of that particular, it has to designate the cause of the individuals composing that class. In other words, that definition should cover not only the characteristics of the class and the universal aspects of its nature, but also give the limits, and defining lines, that distinguish every member of the class, state the reason why they came into being, and that they are so many, and not more. Therefore, he says, "it may be absolutely concluded that everything whose nature involves the existence of a certain number of individuals must of necessity have, since they exist, an external cause": for only an external cause can explain the existence of such a definite number of particular objects in the class. We may add that, if it has to have an external cause, then it cannot be a substance that can exist only in itself, and be known only through itself, as Spinoza deems substance to be. In other words, if there is plurality of being, there must be an external cause for a certain object, it cannot be self-subsistent. And if it is not self-subsistent, it cannot, according to Spinoza, be a substance. For a substance, he says, "is in itself and is conceived through itself."

From this reasoning Spinoza concludes that these particular objects are mere "modes" of that one substance, for a "mode" he defines as that "which is in something else." But to be in something else is basically different from having its efficient cause in something else. The first applies to a "mode," the other to a created reality. Because the one is "in" something else, it has unity of substance and attributes with it; because the other has merely its efficient cause in that other reality, neither its substance nor its attributes are the same. The one is positive and creative, the other is passive in nature. The one is absolute, the other is contingent in being. In short, Spinoza's reasoning in Note 2 proves that there can be only one self-subsisting absolute substance; but that does not preclude the existence of a contingent world as well. And his argument from plurality of being proves that these particular objects are created, just as much as it can prove that they are modes. If the divine nature revealed in the prophets is a "mode" of God, then the fact that so many such prophets have appeared and not more, proves the existence of a law and order dependent upon the Prima Purpose of a transcendent God. But the same argument can be applied to the plurality of the objects of nature, where design and law and order also dominate.

21. THE PRINCIPLE OF GRADATION OF BEING

"The more reality," Spinoza says, "or being a thing has, the more attributes will it have." (Prop. IX) And he considers this principle obvious from Definition 4. But if we follow the principle of emanation, and apply it to all reality, and maintain that there is one substance which necessarily exists, what can we mean by having "more reality or being"? Having one essence, one nature, one definition, and none beside, it should be considered as possessing the same level of reality throughout its substantial expanse. It is only when, under the doctrine of creation, plurality of substance is maintained; when one necessarily exists, and hence is self-subsistent; and another, which has its cause in other than itself, and hence, is created and contingent; that the principle of gradation of being can be discovered. Between a substance, and its "modes" reality is identical and, therefore, there can be no gradation of being. Between a creative substance and the created there is difference of reality which is revealed through their corresponding functions and characteristics. Hence, only in the field of creation can we say difference of substance prevails, that the being of one is Higher and fuller than the other. In short, only under the doctrine of creation, and within its field of operation, gradation of being is realized. In the realm of emanation no such principle can apply without disturbing spiritual and cultural consequences.

The whole edifice of revealed religion, and of the spiritual and cultural life, is based upon two principles: first, the unity of substance and attributes between God and the divine nature revealed in the prophets; and second, the unity of substance and attributes between the divine nature revealed in the different prophets themselves, as manifestations or emanations of God. For, as the Bab would say, they are different rays of the same light, which have emerged from the substance of the same Sun, and reflected in different mirrors, at different periods of human history, and different stages of its development. The image of the transcendent God, the divine Essence and attributes, resides not in the mirror, not in the glass, but in the Sun whose light they reflect. Gradation of being in this realm of emanation impairs the unity of substance and attributes and hence the spiritual and cultural life of man based on it. But it is otherwise in the field of creation.

To a rationalist who views all things from the standpoint of an observer, attributes are "the essence of a substance" (Def. 4); that is, its definition. Ontologically, attributes are types of action and reaction an individual substantial reality reveals; that is, its properties and functions. In the field of creation, these attributes are properties and functions the individual has the capacity of acquiring and, in turn, revealing. In this sense, Baha'u'llah says: "Upon the inmost reality of each and every created thing He hath shed the light of one of His names and made it recepient of the glory of one of His attributes. Upon the reality of man, however, He hath focused the radiance of all His names and attributes, and made it a mirror of His own self. Alone of all created things man hath been singled out for so great a favour, so enduring a bounty" (13).

But we have to stress that the mirror of the human heart has merely the capacity, the capability, of gradually acquiring and then reflecting these divine attributes. Furthermore, man is given freedom of choice, to acquire and reflect these attributes, or disregard them. The result is that there is a variety, both in the composition and measure of mastery, of those attributes, functions and characteristics, and hence, gradation of development in man. And this constitutes the basis of gradation in the world of creation, especially of the human soul, where it is bidden by all the prophets to be regenerated, to be reborn, and arise from the dead.

With such a conception of creation, therefore, we possess different strata of reality and being, revealing different grades of attributes, and different measures of fullness, each can be acquired, practiced and reflected. Man has been chosen, from among all the created things, and endowed with the capacity of acquiring all the divine attributes in the process of his spiritual evolution. And on that ground, he possesses priority of being and reality among created things. But to develop that spiritual and cultural life, he needs the adequate environment, a guiding light, and the necessary stimulant. He needs the vision of those divine attributes put into practice, and in full actuality, that he may be able to conform with them and acquire them. And to the extent he makes those attributes and acquired characteristics his own he grows in reality and being, that is, is reborn and regenerated.

22. THE NATURE OF ATTRIBUTES

"Each attribute of the one substance," says Spinoza, "must be conceived through itself" (Prop. X); and he supports this view with his proof that "an attribute is that which the intellect perceives of a substance as constituting its essence (Def. 4), therefore (Def. 3) it must be conceived through itself."

Having indirectly assailed the principles underlying the doctrine of creation, and to his seeming satisfaction, proven that there is but one substance, which is God's; and having tried to show that what revealed religion considers to be created substances—that is, individual objects, whether spiritual in nature or physical—are merely "modes" of that primary, and unitary, substance; Spinoza now proceeds to state what its attributes are. Taking the view point of what we have considered to be that of a rationalist, and an observer, Spinoza proceeds to state that these attributes must be conceived through themselves, as characteristics which the intellect perceives, and which constitute the essence and definition of the underlying substance. Then in a Note appended to the Proposition, he adds that two attributes may be predicated of the same substance. In other words, that multiplicity of attributes does not necessarily involve multiplicity of substance.

We have already observed that attributes which epistemologically constitute the essence of a substance ontologically are types of action and reaction it reveals. They are functions and properties it reveals and characteristics it expresses in its various types of movements. To appre-

85

ciate an attribute, therefore, we cannot abstract the substance from its environment. That is, what substance is, as it is in itself, is unknowable: it is known only through its relations and interactions with other substances, that is, in the other individual objects. And this principle applies whether the substance be divine and creative, or natural and created. In other words, the multiplicity of the conditions which prevail in the environment draws out, and makes actual, the multiplicity of attributes potential in the object.

Because all the divine attributes spring from the one substance and entity which underlies them all, because they are revelations of the same Primary Purpose, they possess an inner harmony in their form of activity. For it is the same substance, with the same Purpose which reveals itself as the occasions arise and circumstances demand. Though these attributes are seemingly at times contrary, yet they complement one another, in pursuit of a common Purpose, and towards an identical end. For example, God is conceived as avenging, and also as loving, fierce in anger, but also merciful. He reveals these seemingly contrary attributes as circumstances differ, and the same supreme Primary Purpose is made to confront different environments and stages of human development. But these attributes become contradictory and mutually exclusive only when they are made to apply indifferently either to a creator or to a created, when they are made to imply absoluteness or contingency, self-sufficiency and utter reliance; when they are considered both attributes specifically of a "mover," or those of a "moved." For, the same substance may reveal contrary attributes at different occasions, when circumstances differ, but cannot possess contradictory principles within its very unitary being and Purpose. Such primary existential attributes, implying a Creator on the one hand, and a created on the other, necessitate different substances and nature.

For example, the meekness Jesus taught in his sermon on the mount, and which he exemplified on the cross, was contrary to the ruthless severity he practiced in driving out the moneychangers from the Temple grounds; or in his saying: "Think not that I am come to send peace on earth: I am come not to send peace, but a sword" (14). In either case, he revealed divine attributes but they were reactions of the Spirit of God, resident in him, to different environments. They were dictates of the same Primary Purpose, but in different circumstances. Similarly, the revelation of Jesus Christ, and of Mohammed, were seemingly unlike,

86

and advocating different rights and ordinances; but they were both divine in origin, and serving the same spiritual and cultural purpose. Therefore, they were substantially the same, for they were revelations of the same eternal Word of God. On the other hand, man may learn to reveal the same attributes that the prophets manifest in their words and deeds and, like Peter, express the same meekness and self-sacrifice, and like his Master, be crucified on the cross: but yet be substantially different. For the one would reveal those attributes, and the other acquires them; the one is the creator of the spiritual and cultural life, the other a mere recipient of that light.

The same type of substantial difference may be distinguished in the relation of the human soul to the physical body of man. The two are closely associated. The soul and the bodily senses fully cooperate in the pursuit of the same purpose. They feel the same feelings, suffer the same sufferings, and are enthused by the same pleasures. In other words, they both may reveal the same attributes; but according to revealed religion, the spirit acts as the "mover," the bodily senses as the "moved." The one is a free agent, the other a controlled instrument. The one is "natural body," the other "spiritual body," or substance, as Paul put it (15). Therefore, they are substantially different, and cannot be identified. In other words, attributes can be understood only through the Purpose that dominates them.

23. PROOFS FOR THE EXISTENCE OF GOD ADVANCED BY THE DIFFERENT SYSTEMS OF THOUGHT

Every system of thought, whether idealistic, empirical, mystic or religious, has its own peculiar approach in proving the existence of God. Every one of these proofs is based upon the primary premises that system adopts. Therefore, the strength and weakness each possesses depends ultimately upon the hypothetical premises that system has chosen. The idealist approach starts with the hypothesis that ultimate reality, that is, the idea of God, like all other ideas, is innate, and inherent, in the mind of man. And then, with that as a premise, tries to show that such idea necessarily entails existence. The empiricist, on the other hand, begins with the premise that reality resides not in the ideas but in objects of empirical experience. And the "motion," change, or integration we observe in nature, necessitates the existence of an unmoved Mover which is God. Mysticism denies the efficacy of mind in attaining such truths and upholds instead the principle of direct apprehension, or intuition. It bases this method of knowledge upon the fundamental premise that only like can know its like. In other words, at rare moments of ecstacy, the human soul feels itself one with God, and thereby acquires certainty of its substantial oneness with Him, and hence, of His existence, and of the veracity of that experience. Revealed religion considers these basic premises of the different systems of thought all faulty, and therefore, denies the absolute efficacy of the proofs they try to support, and the truths they try to establish. Instead, it stresses the principle of revelation as the only basis for attaining certainty regarding the existence of God, and the veracity of the attributes of perfection predicated of Him. It maintains that existence is first detected through His creative power, and purpose, manifest in the constant and eternal integration of the physical universe, and then, in the evolution of the spiritual and cultural life of man. Secondly, through His specific act of grace, when He reveals His Primal Purpose, and attributes of perfection, through the divine nature of the prophets, and their words and deeds, the existence of His divine being is established.

24. SPINOZA'S PROOFS FOR THE EXISTENCE OF GOD

"God," Spinoza says, "or a substance consisting of infinite attributes, each of which expresses eternal and infinite essence, necessarily exists" (Prop. XI); and his proof for that existence is that "if you deny it, conceive, if it is possible, that God does not exist. Then (Ax. 7) his essence does not involve existence. But this (Prop. 7) is absurd. Therefore God necessarily exists."

Spinoza, we have observed, was heir to the Neoplatonic principle of divine emanation, which was blended with Greek rationalism, and the mystic principle of substantial unity of the human soul and God. Whereas the Proposition of Spinoza is positive, that is, starts from the essence of God, and then tries to show the necessity of His existence, his proof for that proposition tends to be negative in nature. In other words, he tries to establish his argument by showing the absurdity of the alternative principle, namely, that God does not exist. He thus tries to modify the positive idealistic and rationalistic assertion that ultimate reality resides in the idea, and that the idea of God, being supremely real, necessarily entails existence, which is an affirmative procedure of reasoning, by disproving the contrary. He employs the negative method, at times used in geometry. We cannot conceive God, the supreme Idea man entertains as basis of all his thought, as not existing; therefore, we are constrained to maintain that He exists. But to deny the contrary is a very weak way of asserting the positive alternative. Furthermore, in the case of the other attributes of God, such as love, mercy, wisdom, justice and beauty, a negative method of reasoning completely fails. For the spiritual and cultural life of man needs positive values and examples, which can become definite objects of contemplation and understanding on the part of man. Otherwise he cannot be drawn to them, practice them, and gradually acquire them. The words and deeds of Jesus and Mohammed helped the spiritual and cultural evolution of man because they were positive examples of the divine attributes humanity had to acquire.

In the same trend is Spinoza's second proof for the existence of God. "That must of necessity exist," he says, "concerning which no reason or cause is granted which could prevent its existence. If thus no reason or cause can be granted which could prevent the existence of God or take his existence from him, it must certainly be concluded that he does exist of necessity." Spinoza argues that there should be a reason why a thing exists, or why it ceases to be. Further, that cause, or reason, may be internal and immanent in that object, or external and transcendent to it. According to Proposition 7, he says, existence is inherent in the very nature of substance; therefore, if there is any cause or reason to be assigned for substance, it should be internal to it. Hence with God, who is self-subsisting, substance exists of necessity in Him.

In his third proof, Spinoza argues that existence is a form of power, a power to be. If finite objects have existence, they have power to be. How can we, therefore, maintain that an infinite reality has less existence than finite things? "Therefore, either nothing exists, or a being absolutely infinite necessarily exists." As then he proceeds to show the more its attributes of perfection, the fuller the existence of that reality. In other words, a being that is absolute in its perfections is also absolute in its being.

25. THE IDEALISTIC PROOF WOULD BETTER APPLY TO THE DIVINE NATURE REVEALED IN THE PROPHETS

The idealistic proof for the existence of God, namely, to deduce from the conception of His essence that of His existence; or, from any attribute to its perfection, full actuality, and absolute form; all possess their measure of validity; but, according to revealed religion, they can be adequately appreciated only in the light of revelation, that is, only if applied to the divine nature revealed in the prophets. For, God being absolutely transcendent in essence and attributes of perfection, is utterly beyond human understanding, and beyond the grasp of feeling, intuition and inner experiences, as rationalists and mystics respectively maintain.

Revealed religion fully confirms the principle that essence, when applied to God, involves existence. For existence can be considered separate only when taken as a prelude to a project and creative process. In that case, essence is of an inchoate reality, viewed as a sketch in the mind of the creator, and, as such, is devoid of substantiality. But in such a case, it applies solely to contingent beings, and constitutes the ground of their constant change, in the process of their evolution. For creation signifies to conceive the essence, or attributes, functions and qualities an object ought to possess and then mold them into some material to generate an individual being. An absolute reality, that is, an unmoved Mover, transcends such a generative process; hence, its essence or attributes, whatever they may be, are inherent in its very being.

But, as the divine nature revealed in the prophets is substantially one with God and hence, attributes of perfection, in their full actuality, reside and inhere in it; further, because those attributes, through the words and deeds of the prophet, become empirical objects of human understanding; it is more factual to say that in the prophets essence conforms with existence. When referred to the prophets this principle neither impairs the doctrine of divine transcendence nor leaves the source, and objective validity, of the divine attributes uncertain. To a human "observer," only the image in the mirror has positive being. The original source of the image in the mirror has positive being. The original source of the image is beyond the scope of his vision. And reference back to it, is bound to be an inference.

But the basic problem which confronts the religious life is not only whether God exists; but whether all the divine attributes we predicate of Him possess objective reference and validity. Existence is only one of the infinite attributes we predicate of Him. It is the possibility of knowledge of divine perfections, which constitutes the object and purpose of religious thought. In other words, it is how can we establish the objective validity of the perfections we predicate of God, when we premise that in

His essence He absolutely transcends human understanding and power of intuition and so-called mystic experiences. The error of Idealism was to start with the hypothesis that such an essence is an idea innate in the mind of the generality of mankind, of even a slave-boy, as Plato tries to prove. As we have repeatedly stressed, according to revealed religion, these ideas are not innate in the mind of man, for he merely acquires them through education. They are innate solely in the mind of the prophets; or rather, in the divine nature revealed in the prophets, acting as creator of man's spiritual and cultural life. For that divine nature is substantially one with God; and, as such, can constitute the ontological ground for that knowledge and understanding. Even the purely human nature of the prophets fails to grasp the full essence of God and His attributes; for this human nature is, as already observed, a created reality; and a created reality cannot understand the nature of its creator. "So perfect and comprehensive is His creation," says Baha'u'llah, "that no mind nor heart however keen or pure, can ever grasp the nature of the most insignificant of His creatures, much less fathom the mystery of Him Who is the Day Star of Truth, Who is the invisible and unknowable Essence. The conception of the devoutest of mystics, the attainments of the most accomplished amongst men, the highest praise which human tongue or pen can render are all the product of man's finite mind and are conditioned by its limitations. Ten thousand Prophets, each a Moses, are thunderstruck upon the Sinai of their search at His forbidding voice, 'Thou shalt never behold Me!'; whilst a myriad Messengers, each as great as Jesus, stand dismayed upon their heavenly thrones by the interdiction, 'Mine Essence thou shalt never apprehend!' " (16).

If man cannot claim to possess a knowledge and understanding of the essence of God, that is, a definition of His transcendent nature and reality, then it is idle to proceed and maintain that God's essence involves necessary existence, or to seek from Him the spiritual and cultural values and forms. The utmost man can claim is that were he to possess an understanding of God's essence—which is admittedly absolutely impossible—then he would of necessity have to deduce from it God's existence as well. For in the case of an absolute reality, which is premised to be self-subsistent, and has the cause of its being in itself, essence and existence, a quality and its full actuality, cannot be conceived apart and separate.

91

26. SIMILARLY THE EMPIRICAL PROOF WOULD BETTER APPLY TO THE DIVINE NATURE REVEALED IN THE PROPHETS

In the Bayan, the Bab says that, upon every object God has shed the sign or trace of His being, with which that object can glorify Him and, in that sense, worship Him. (17). When we remember the Bab states further that the transcendent reality of God created the Primal Purpose and made it the expression of His Essence (18); and, through it, generated the universe, including the spiritual and cultural life of man; we conclude that it is His creative will and purpose which has so dominated all things not His substance and reality. If man should center his attention on the glass, the Bab says, the image reflected in the mirror will elude his attention; for he would not see but the glass. But if he direct his attention upon the image, then the mirror, and its material significance will vanish. For it will be the image alone which will be then brought into relief and observed. Similarly, if man should focus his attention upon the "sign," or trace of God's nature, which is His creative purpose, in the spiritual and cultural life of man, it is only that Purpose which will be dominant. All else would seem insignificant and irrelevant to its understanding. Man would then see no traces of physical matter but only the Primal Purpose of God, creating, sustaining, causing death, and imparting a new life.

In no field of the empirical world is that truth as clearly and distinctly brought out as in man's spiritual and cultural life, where the Primal Purpose operates through the prophets. To a discerning mind, the whole of human culture and spiritual life will be then throbbing with the creative, sustaining, and life-giving power of God, and thereby constitute the sphere from which man should collect his empirical data for verifying his proof for the existence of God. But that verification will establish, not the existence, sovereignty, wisdom and dominion of the transcendent God; but rather of His Primal Purpose, as manifested through the divine nature revealed in the prophets. In other words, the empirical proof for the existence of God would better apply to the divine nature of the prophets than to the transcendent God Himself.

27. THE MYSTIC CLAIM TO INTUITIVE EXPERIENCE OF GOD'S PRESENCE WOULD ALSO BETTER APPLY TO THE DIVINE NATURE REVEALED IN THE PROPHETS

The proof for the existence of God, held by mystics, may be boiled down to two basic principles, one of being, another of knowledge. First, it premises unity of substance between the human soul and God. Secondly, it maintains that "like can know its like": that unity of substance imparts unity of consciousness and of thought. This knowledge, however, is not discursive but rather in the nature of an inner experience and intuitive. It is essentially direct, and a form of contemplation and immediate apprehension. Now, on what ground can we say that this knowledge would better apply to the divine nature revealed in the prophets, and constitute a proof of God's existence?

We have already observed the Bab stress that the sea of divine nature does not enter the sea of created being; nor the sea of created being enter the sea of divine nature. (19) These two worlds are in substance absolutely different, and therefore apart, except that the one is the Creator, and the other the created. In other words, according to the Bab, there is neither unity of substance, nor a ground for the principle of "like can know its like" to operate. According to revealed religion, this is a fact which no man can gainsay. For, no matter how much the mystic may strive, he can never show a sign that he has actually attained intuitive knowledge of that objective reality, and enjoyed inner experience with it. In other words, he cannot infer objective validity from his subjective experience. And the proof that he has not attained to them is that he cannot produce a fruit that would possess value for the spiritual and cultural life of man. His attainment seems as barren as anything can be.

Unity of substance, we have observed, prevails, according to revealed religion, between God and the divine nature revealed in the prophets. Hence, the knowledge possessed by these is not discursive, but immediate. It is in the nature of a direct inner experience, a sort of "like knowing its like," intuitive and certain. And the proof that this knowledge is true and God's is that upon it has stood the spiritual and cultural life of humanity down the ages. It has not been barren, such as the one claimed by the mystics; but an infinite source of Wisdom, acting as mainspring of all spiritual and cultural values, needed for human regeneration and rebirth.

Furthermore, we have observed that the divine nature revealed in the prophets acts as an image, reflected in their human nature, operating as a mirror. It is the Primal Purpose revealing the fullness of the divine attributes of perfection. It is the divine Essence manifesting itself in a manner accessible to human knowledge and understanding. Being such, the divine nature revealed in the prophets is the actual object of contemplation, and direct apprehension; rather than of inference, and hypothetical assertions. While the divine Substance and Essence are absolutely transcendent to human thought, the divine nature revealed in the prophets, their words and deeds, constitutes the supreme object of human intellect. Coming in contact with that reality, and moved by its creative purpose, mankind has evolved spiritually and culturally down the ages. Its recurring appearances has brought about the seasonal springtime of individual and social regeneration and rebirth. And the history of the human race bears ample witness to it. For the appearance of Moses constitutes the supreme event in the cultural history of the Hebrews, and stands as a clear and distinct phenomenon for the historian to study and appreciate. The same is true of the advent of Jesus, Zoroaster and Mohammed, in the culture they have each generated in their respective age. They are outstanding events, clear and distinct, for empirical verification. In short, mystic experience, direct contemplation of the divine Essence, becomes veridical and efficacious, not if the object of that experience and contemplation be identified with the transcendent God, but rather when applied to the divine nature revealed in the prophets. And only then will that knowledge produce its spiritual and cultural fruits. In short, according to the Bab and Baha'u'llah, the right experience of "divine presence" empirically applies to the presence of these prophets on earth.

28. THE NEGATIVE METHOD EMPLOYED BY SPINOZA RENDERS HIS PROOFS LESS EFFECTIVE

If the conceptions substance, essence and existence can be identified in the divine nature revealed in the prophets; if we admit as empirical truth that the spiritual and cultural life of man is a phenomenon revealing God's Primal Purpose and creative activity, pursued through the prophets; if the divine Presence, which is the supreme occasion for communion with God on earth, which the mystics hope for, is realized and positively experienced at the advent of the prophets in the world and in human society; then we have no reason to fall back on the negative method of reasoning, followed by Spinoza, to prove the existence of God. Being attributed to the prophets, who are one in substance with God, and hence unmoved Movers and Absolute, in nature and being, we feel under logical necessity to admit that these ideas such as wisdom, love and sovereignty, or essences, involve being and existence. For, besides the empirical and historical evidence which support our assertion, the qualities we attribute to the prophets, as instruments of God's creative Purpose, are qualities they reveal out of their own nature, which is the perfect and unchanging nature and substance of God Himself.

In other words, the idealistic proof for the existence of God, whether in its positive form, as Descartes presented it; or in the negative one, as Spinoza chose as his method of reasoning; both acquire their validity and objectivity, only on condition that the "idea" or "essence" of God is rendered an object of human understanding, through His self-revelation. For both Descartes and Spinoza, in true rationalistic method of procedure, start with "essence" and try to deduce from it "existence." While from a factually unknowable "essence" no valid "existence" can be logically deduced. To presume that the divine essence is knowable, to make that the premise of our thought is to vitiate all our reasoning, and its result is that "existence" becomes hypothetical as well. Only after accepting the divine nature of the prophets, as revelation of the substance of God, would the idealistic proof, adopted by Spinoza, obtain significance and validity. For only then will the "essence," or attributes and nature of God, become positive objects of human understanding. It is on this ground that Baha'u'llah says that the divine nature and reality of the prophets constitute the basis on which proofs of the existence of God obtain validity and acquire significance.

Thus, the proofs of Spinoza are inversions of three positive ones, advanced for the existence of God, but which acquire their validity only if applied to the principle of revelation. The first is from essence to being, which, we observed, becomes object of human understanding when applied to the divine nature revealed in the prophets. The second is an inference from contingency to absolute being and actuality, which is verifiable, when we compare the values man has to acquire in the process of his spiritual and cultural evolution, with the full perfections prophets manifest through their words and deeds. The third proof is based upon the principle that God's attributes of perfection entail their existence; for nothing can be considered as perfect if not in being. Without the prophets, and their manifestation of those attributes, the process becomes anthropomorphic, and an idle fancy of human imagination and hopes. For how can we predicate a certain quality to God if He is transcendent and unknowable? In short, without the revelation, vouchsafed through the prophets, the basic premise of all these proofs, namely, knowledge of the nature of God's essence, and attributes, can never be established and verified.

29. INDIVIDUATION AS DIVISION INTO PARTS

When the universe, or "the All," is identified with God, that is, when unity of substance is maintained, then individuation can be conceived only through the process of division or addition. And the fundamental principle of division and addition is that they can apply only to objects which are in substance and attributes alike. These mathematical processes cannot operate among dissimilar objects. Unlike things cannot be added; and a uniform substance cannot be divided into dissimilar things. To pagan Greeks, who set aside the principle of creation as understood by revealed religion, and maintained the doctrine of monism, and emanation of all being from God, division and addition could be considered as the only possible processes of individuation. And being a monist, and pantheist, Spinoza was naturally led to that belief.

"No attribute of a substance," says Spinoza, "can be truly conceived, from which it would follow that substance can be divided into parts" (Prop. XII). To prove this proposition Spinoza maintains that the substance so divided into parts will have either to retain its original nature or not retain it. If it does retain it, then every substance so produced will be, like the original one, infinite (Prop. 8); will act as its own cause, that is, be self-subsisting (Prop. 6) and nevertheless, possess different attributes (Prop. 5). And that is absurd. Because, according to Spinoza's previous reasonings, there cannot be more than one infinite substance that is self-subsisting. Nor can these possess the same nature and substance, but different attributes. For as we have already observed, difference of attributes denotes difference of substance. On the other hand, if we maintain that the parts do not retain the same nature and attributes, the original substance will lose its substantiality completely, and cease to exist. And this in the light of Prop. 7 is absurd.

30. INDIVIDUATION, AS A RESULT OF DIVISION, IS APPLIC-ABLE ONLY WITHIN THE SPHERE OF EMANATION

The problem of individuation, which Spinoza tries to tackle in this proposition, is the logical outcome of the doctrine of unity of substance and its emanation into objects which are of similar substance and attributes. For, if all things are mere "offshoot," or "overflow," or "radiation" of the same primordial reality, constituting one homogeneous "universe;" if they are all of the same substance though projected into different "modes" of being; if they are "appearances" of the same reality; then on what ground would their individuation stand, except on division and addition? Under the doctrines of unity of substance, and of emanation, individuation as a process, producing different substances possessing different attributes, has no ontological ground. When the human soul, and objects of nature, are considered mere "modes" of the same substance, as Spinoza conceived them to be, individuation as generation of separate substances possessing separate attributes consti-tutes a major problem to be resolved. And it cannot be resolved without involving basic contradictions, as Spinoza's reasoning shows.

31. INDIVIDUATION AS GENERATION OF DIFFERENT SUB-STANCES, WITH DIFFERENT ATTRIBUTES, IS THE OUTCOME OF THE PROCESS OF CREATION

Just as the mathematical processes of addition and division necessitate unity of substance and attributes between the original object and the product and therefore apply fully to the principle of emanation, so does the process of creation, which is synthetic, require difference of con-stituting elements, and difference between these and the catalyzer, which is the dominating creative purpose. And the reason for it is that here individuation is not merely numerical and matter of magnitude, but also essential and formal, that is, substantial and qualitative. The Creator and the created cannot be added together to constitute a class called "the all;" nor can an "all" be divided into such dissimilar entities as a creator and a created, or of created objects of different grades of being, possessing different forms and properties and attributes. And if difference of form and attributes is admitted, they cannot be considered substantially the same.

Thus, just as the understanding of an observer seeks the universal idea, or form, and formulates it as a general conception; so does creative activity generate the individual, and sustains its being and evolution. Therefore, any system of thought which tries to set aside the principle of creation, as maintained by revealed religion, and instead attempts to explain the existence of the human soul and objects of physical nature through the doctrine of emanation, is logically led to set aside the principle of individuation, or minimize its significance. And Spinoza was led to that tendency in his proposition.

32. SPINOZA'S ARGUMENT APPLIES TO THE DIVINE NATURE REVEALED IN THE PROPHETS

We said that revealed religion restricts the sphere of the operation of the principle of emanation to that of revelation; and hence, to the divine nature revealed in the prophets. The result of such an outlook is that the principle of divine unity like other attributes of perfection is not impaired, notwithstanding the plurality of its manifestations. Unity, like plurality, is essentially a category of human understanding; hence it cannot, strictly speaking, be applied to the nature of an absolutely transcendent reality such as God. God absolutely transcends those categories, because he absolutely transcends human thought and understanding. Therefore, strictly speaking, Divine Unity applies to revelation: first, to unity between the substance of God and His revelations; secondly, to the unity of the different revelations, in substance, purpose and attributes; in other words, unity of the divine nature revealed in all the prophets that have appeared down the ages. It was on this ground, of unity of revelation, that John said referring to the reality of Jesus Christ: "In the beginning was the Word, and the Word was with God, and the Word was God." The Word was an emanation of the divine substance which, from ancient of days, appeared in the prophets, and maintained their substantial unity with God. On the same ground Christ foretold his own advent in ages to come, and under circumstances, time, and locality, utterly different. Mohammed put this principle of divine unity, in both its aspects, far more emphatically when he said in the Koran: "Verily those who believe not in God and His Messengers; and separate between God and His Messengers; and say we believe in some, and in some we believe not; and desire to take a middle way; these are veritable infidels; and for the infidels we have prepared a shameful punishment. And they who believe in God and His Messengers, and do not make any difference between them, on these we shall bestow a reward"(20). Here Mohammed stresses both aspects of divine Unity: that between God and His prophets, and also that between the prophets themselves. And that unity involves unity of substance and attributes.

33. THE BAB ON THE PRINCIPLE OF DIVISION, AS THE PROCESS OF INDIVIDUATION

Let us consider the example of the primary mirrors, mentioned by the Bab in the Bayan as referring to the prophets, and the secondary mirrors, standing for the "Valis," or successors of the prophets in the leadership and guidance of the followers of the Faith after them, and then of the believers. The light of God, which is shed upon the human nature of the prophets as primary mirror might be considered as "division"; for such radiation does not impair the quality, unity and substantiality, of the light emanating from the sun, or, in turn, from the primary mirrors, as projected upon the secondary mirrors, or humanity at large. Though this light is diffused throughout all the universe, and from eternity to eternity, it is always the same light in quality and substance: the same light of God, representing His primary Purpose, and creating the spiritual and cultural life of man, as its supreme objective.

34. BAHA'U'LLAH ON THE UNITY OF THE DIVINE NATURE REVEALED IN THE PROPHETS, AND THE PLURALITY OF THEIR HUMAN NATURE

Baha'u'llah deals in detail with the two natures which combine in the prophets; and while he stresses the unity which characterises their divine nature, shows how individuality and plurality is expressed in their human aspect, that is, the nature they possess in common with the generality of mankind, and which is, not an emanation, but a creation of God. "These manifestations of God," says Baha'u'llah, "have each a twofold station. One is the station of pure abstraction and essential unity. In this respect, if thou callest them all by one name, and dost ascribe to them the same attributes, thou hast not erred from the truth. Even as he hath revealed: 'No distinction do we make between any of His Messengers'. . . . Thus hath Mohammed the Point of the Qur'an revealed: 'I am all the prophets.' Likewise, He saith: 'I am the first Adam, Noah, Moses and Jesus'. . . . The other station is the station of distinction, and pertains to the world of creation, and to the limitations thereof. In this respect, each manifestation of God hath a distinct individuality, and definitely prescribed mission, a predestined revelation, and specially designed limitations. Each one of them is characterized by a special attribute, fulfils a definite mission, and is entrusted with a particular Revelation. . . ."(21).

In short, in so far as the divine nature revealed in the prophets is an emanation of God, unity of the divine Substance is not impaired. All the prophets are, on the one hand, substantially one with God, and on the other, substantially one among themselves. It is due to this substantial unity between them and God that the spiritual and cultural life of man is considered divine in origin. And it is due to the substantial unity between the prophets that that spiritual and cultural life is one in origin, one in purpose, and one in goal and aim, though revealed in far distant ages, and far differing environments and circumstances. Therefore, only when restricted to the field of emanation of the divine nature revealed in the prophets is Spinoza's proposition true, and spiritually and culturally sound and fruitful.

35. SPINOZA'S PROPOSITION FAILS TO APPLY TO THE WORLD OF CREATION

But this doctrine of "division," as process of individuation, which is characteristic of the field of emanation, fails completely, both ontologically, and also spiritually and culturally, when applied to the sphere of the world of creation. For between the two, the Creator and the created, there can be no substantial unity. As Baha'u'llah says: "Consider the relation between the craftsman and his handiwork, between the painter and his painting. Can it ever be maintained that the work their hands have produced is the same as themselves? By Him Who is the Lord of the Throne above and of the earth below! They can be regarded in no other light except as evidence that proclaim the excellence and perfection of their author" (22). Thus, there can be no substantial unity between the Creator and the created, between God and the human soul, and much less between Him and objects of physical nature. These are the products of a different form of proceeding from God. They are not emanations, but creations. They are not parts "divided" from the divine substance; but handiworks of His Primal Purpose.

As creation is giving a new form to a specific material to generate a new higher individual substance, with new functions and attributes; the process is synthetic in nature, rather than mere division or fission, or radiation. And the divine Primal Purpose operates as the catalyzer. This

Primal Purpose remains transcendent and beyond both, the constituting elements and the resulting substance, just as every creator is to the object he creates, like an artisan to his work of art. The Primal Purpose guides and directs the mutual action and reaction of the constituting element, the matter and the form, from its position of eminence as creator.

Thus, being a created reality, the human soul possesses an individuality inherent in its being—an individuality which, through repeated generation, and constant reintegration, is developed and enhanced, rather than reduced and overcome. And this basic ontological individuality gives purpose and meaning to the spiritual and cultural life which man leads, and to the perfections he gradually acquires and accumulates as eternal treasures which he carries into the world to come.

36. THE PREDICAMENTS THAT ARISE WHEN THE PRINCIPLE OF DIVISION IS PHYSICALLY INTERPRETED AND UNIVERSALLY APPLIED

In Proposition 13 Spinoza says that "substance absolutely infinite is indivisible." To prove it he says that if an infinite absolute substance be divided, its parts will either retain the nature of the original substance, or lose it. If they retain it, then there would result a plurality of substances, all having the same nature and attributes. And that is absurd; for, according to Prop. 5, there cannot be two or more substances, all having the same nature and attributes. If, on the other hand, these parts lose the nature of the original substance, this latter will cease to exist. But, according to Prop. 7, that is absurd; for a substance exists necessarily, and hence cannot be destroyed.

That absolute infinite substance, that is, the divine nature, is indivisible, is a logical outcome of the doctrine of emanation, and the form of proceeding from God, which leaves His substantial unity unimpaired. God's substance cannot be said to be divided into the divine nature of so many prophets, just as the sun cannot be said to be divided into so many mirrors which happen to reflect its light; if by division is meant a physical phenomenon, and a geometrical method of segmentation of a line. For a line or angle ceases to be of a definite measure if divided and segmented into parts. Division is a category of human understanding applicable to physical objects; it cannot, strictly speaking, be applied to a reality which is in substance spiritual. Hitherto, when we have spoken of addition or division regarding the nature of proceeding from God it was merely to stress one aspect of it, namely, that it did not impare unity of substance, as creation does. For division and addition can be only between realities which are substantially alike. There is no universal human soul, segmented into individual ones, as a line is into its parts, for it is a creation and not an emanation of God. But the premise of Spinoza, which identified God with the physical universe, entailed such a predicament. It extended the doctrine of emanation to include all things, and thus confuse those realities essentially spiritual with others that are essentially physical and material. As a result of such a confusion, purely spiritual entities became subject to physical categories of being and becoming. He did not confine the doctrine of emanation to the divine reality revealed in the prophets, as revealed religion does; that is, maintain it on a purely spiritual level, where physical categories do not apply. In fact, in his corollary to this proposition, he extends this principle to "corporal substance" as well; for he says: "From this it follows that no substance, and consequently no corporeal substance, in so far as it is substance, can be divided into parts." To remain true to his basic monism, and the unity of substance it maintains, he denies a positive category of human understanding applicable to physical being, as basis of individuation.

In short, when we spoke of division, and applied it to the divine nature revealed in the prophets, which is an utterly spiritual reality, and compared it to radiation, and divine overflow, we did not take it as a physical and material process, as Spinoza did. For as a physical process, it entails limitations of the original substance, and its subjection to defining lines; while as a purely spiritual process, it leaves that infinity unimpaired. Spinoza's identification of the substance of the physical, and the spiritual, entailed such difficulties. For though individuality in corporeal things is empirically valid, no logical ground is given for it.

37. CREATION DOES NOT IMPAIR THE INFINITY OF THE CREATOR

In a note appended to this proposition, Spinoza attempts to further strengthen his argument by stating that "part" implies finiteness and this characteristic is inapplicable to substance, which has been shown to be necessarily infinite. Because Spinoza conceived division as a geometrical process applicable to physical entities its result was conceived as physical "parts." And the conception of "part" generated for him a problem and a seeming contradiction.

(For an implied finiteness came to be attributed to substance, which by definition is infinite.) In other words, because he identified the universe, and its physical nature, with God and hence conceived the process of division as physical, the result of his reasoning was physical objects, or "parts," defined by physical defining lines. But if God should be conceived as a purely spiritual reality, absolutely transcendent to all physical categories of being and processes, then its emanations could not be considered as "parts" with defining lines that would limit also His reality. Neither the divine substance, nor its different emanations, would, in that case, lose its infiniteness. In fact the infinity of the one will necessarily imply the infinity of the other. The same is true if the relation between God and the universe, including physical nature, is regarded as that of creator and created.

Spinoza ends his note stating that: "finite substance," that is "part," "involves an obvious contradiction." But why should there be such a contradiction if the process does not involve emanation, but is limited to creation; even when the product of the process is to generate "finite substance," which is individual? To revert to the example used by Baha'u'llah and quoted above, an artisan or painter can never be considered as divided between his artifacts and paintings; nor can these be considered as "parts" of his nature and being. And as they are not "parts" of his being they cannot set limits and defining lines to His nature and substance. In fact, the infinity of His productions is the best proof for the infinity of His creative power and purpose.

Just as it is anthropomorphic and disparaging to attribute to God, who is an absolute, transcendent reality, characteristics specifically human, and categories of being that are essentially creaturely; so it is devoid of sense, and detrimental to man's spiritual and cultural growth, to predicate of man relations prevailing between God and His prophets. For the one is a creation of God, with perfections to be acquired; while the other is an emanation, already in full actuality and perfection. Creation, if considered as "improvement," as acquiring of perfections, is the integration of an individual entity into a higher state of being. Its counterpart is disintegration, when the sustaining purpose of God, that is, the integrating process, is not positively operative. This is the field of natural phenomenon to which propositions 12 and 13 apply, in case the expression "substance absolutely infinite" is taken to denote both the natural and the divine; for division into parts is disintegration: what the Bab terms

103

"death." The reality of the process of "death," that is, of disintegration, is as negative as the process of "creation, sustenance and imparting life" mentioned by the Bab, is positive. None of these can be denied, as characteristic of the world of creation, and the spiritual and cultural life of mankind. Just as there are periods of cultural growth, there are seasons of cultural setback, "death," and decay. History records both as positive experiences of mankind throughout the ages. We cannot deny this historical fact on the ground that divine substance is indivisible, that the world of nature, being in substance divine, cannot be subject to disintegration. The principle, while figuratively applicable to the divine nature revealed in the prophets, becomes senseless when extended to the field of creation, including the spiritual and cultural life of man, where "death" is an outstanding phenomenon, put by the Bab alongside with sustenance and giving life. Integration and disintegration are characteristic of the "moved," just as much as transcendence to them is characteristic of the "Mover." We cannot confuse the two realms, of being and of becoming, and yet speak sense, and not endanger the spiritual and cultural life of man. In short, by identifying the spiritual and the physical, or rather, by considering them both as "modes" of the same universal divine Reality, Spinoza made categories of physical being, such as unity and plurality, addition and division, applicable to God as well; and thus, lead to insurmountable difficulties and predicaments.

The Bab, we have observed, considers the divine Essence inaccessible to human thought, and as Creator, absolutely transcendent to the world of creation. He created the Primal Purpose, and through it created the physical universe, and the spiritual and cultural life of man. We cannot, on that ground, say that, the Primal Purpose, which is manifested through the prophets, acting as mirror, is divided and segmented into parts as a line would be. The Primal Purpose retains its infiniteness in that operation. In fact, the eternity and expanse of its creative power proves how limitless it is. But though the Primal Purpose is infinite in substance and indivisible, the objects of its creator are individual and finite.

38. SPINOZA'S GROUNDS FOR MONISM

"Except God," Spinoza says, "no substance can be granted or conceived" (Prop. 14). And he bases his proof for this proposition on (a) that God is absolutely infinite; (b) that He expresses the essence of infinite attributes (Def. 6); and (c) that He necessarily exists (Prop. 11). He further states that, if the existence of any other substance were to be admitted, then there would be two substances, possessing the same attributes, and that is absurd (Prop. 5). Hence, no other substance than God can be conceived or considered as existent. Spinoza then adds two corollaries to this proof; namely, first, that God is "alone," and there is "none like Him," hence, only one substance can be granted which is infinite; secondly, that, "extension and thought are either attributes of God or modifications of attributes of God."

(a) We have already observed that the absolute infinity of God and the absolute infinity of the world of creation, when taken in the light of the teachings of revealed religion, far from being contradictory, complement each other both conceptually and existentially. For how can there be a "Mover" without a "moved," a creator without a created? These are not contradictory terms, or processes of being. The one is necessary for the very essence of the definition of the other, and constitutes the ground of its specific function and reality. Therefore, there can be no "infinite creator," without premising an "infinite creation"; and no "infinite creation" without an "infinite Creator." It is absurd to maintain the existence of two infinite substances on the ground that they are mutually exclusive and contradictory; only when they are both regarded as extended, or identified with "extension," as Spinoza does; in other words, when they are both considered as belonging to the same level of being, either in the world of creation, or in the substance of God Himself considered as identical with nature. (Cor. 2) For extension is a category of physical being; and when God is made subject to or identified with extension, He is reduced to the same level of being as physical nature. And on the same level of being, two infinite substances cannot coexist or be conceived as such. But it is otherwise under the doctrine of creation, when God is considered absolutely beyond the world of creation, when, as the Bab says, the sea of divine being does not enter the sea of creation, not the sea of creation enter the ocean of divine being. Therefore, in the light of revealed religion we can say that God is infinite in the sense that "He absolutely transcends extension" while nature is infinite in the sense that it is subject to an extension that can be indefinitely projected.

(b) To establish the ground of his belief in pantheism, Spinoza then proceeds to the attributes of God, and maintains that two substances cannot be conceived as different when their attributes are the same. But here also no necessary contradiction is implied, if nature is considered a creation of God, and not an emanation of His nature; that is, when God and nature are considered on different levels of existence. For though the human soul is regarded as possessing an infinite capacity to reflect the divine attributes of perfection, yet it is a creation of God, contingent, and not part of His sea of being. No matter how accurately a mirror may reflect the sun it can never go beyond the limits of its receptiveness and passivity. In other words, the human soul can never become self-sufficient, and transcend creation, the need for sustenance, the peril of death, and the possibility of fuller life: characteristics the Bab mentions for the world of creation. In contrast, when the two entities are considered on the same level of being, and at the same time, having the same attributes of perfection, then they constitute the same substance, or modes of the same substance. In that case they neither are, nor can be conceived as separate and different. And such is the case only between God and His emanations, or manifestations, in different ages through the divine nature revealed in them all.

(c) The third point Spinoza mentions as ground for monism, is that only one substance can be considered as existing necessarily. While dealing with Proposition 11, we stated that revealed religion never maintains that created substance, like the divine, exists necessarily. We have already observed that matter and form are intellectual abstractions. Expressed as an intellectual formula, form is a mere sketch or pattern for creative activity. In that case they both possess inchoate existence. Ontologically substantial existence pertains solely to the individual, whether that be a human soul, or a physical being. But an essential characteristic of all natural entities is that they move. And the efficient cause of that motion is attributed to God. Hence, their existence cannot be necessary, in the sense of being absolute. They possess mere contingent existence. But that existence is nevertheless real and positive. In fact, God's creative power and purpose is to the extent that the world of creation, whether physical or spiritual, is positive and real, to the extent they are created, sustained, permitted to die, and resuscitated. If the individuality of the human soul and the objects of physical nature were, as some schools of thought deem them to be, unreal, then God's creative, sustaining and resuscitating power would be unreal as well.

106

39. UNREALITY ATTRIBUTED TO EARTHLY EXISTENCE IS RELATIVE

The different Scriptures of revealed religion abound with statements which refer to earthly existence as ephemeral, unreal and deceptive in its pleasures. But this should be interpreted as only relative to the higher stages of existence man is destined to attain, and the purpose he is to fulfill. For an essential feature of a purpose is that its end imparts significance to the different stages of its process of realization. Relative to that good, or goal, man's earthly existence is a passing feature. Compared to the high purpose he is destined to fulfill, worldly pleasures are insignificant. The worth of earthly existence is merely as an indispensable stage in pursuit of that goal and is measured by the extent it furthers its full realization. Therefore, it is only in comparison to the spiritual attainments of man that material existence and physical pleasure are unreal. Just as it is in relation to human requirements in this life that embryonic stages of development obtain significance. But notwithstanding that relative significance, the life of the embryo is real and substantial, and of far-reaching consequences. In this relative sense alone can we say that human existence upon this earthly plane is unreal. It is because its purpose leads to some reality beyond: a stage of existence far superior. Under the doctrine of emanation a reality either exists or not; but with the principle of creation, and its progressive stages of development, reality obtains a relative but increasing significance: a relative death and life. It is in this relative sense that Baha'u'llah says: "The world is but a show, vain and empty, a mere nothing, bearing the resemblance of reality. Set not your affections upon it. Break not the bond that uniteth you with your Creator, and be not of those that have erred and strayed from His ways. . . . It may, moreover, be likened unto a lifeless image of the beloved whom the lover hath sought and found in the end, after long search and to his utmost regret, to be such as cannot 'fatten or appease hunger' " (23). What is the life of an embryo when compared to that of an accomplished man?

40. SPINOZA IDENTIFIES GOD WITH THE UNIVERSE OF MATTER AND MIND

Spinoza appends two corollaries to Proposition 14, both of which bring out the conclusions to which his reasoning logically leads; first, that

"God is one alone, i.e., there is none like him"; secondly, that "extension and thought are either attributes of God or modifications of attributes of God." In other words, to reverse the order of the corollaries, he considers all objects of the physical universe, and the human soul, which he identifies with thought, or mind, as substantially one with God. And then, having identified the substance of all things with His nature, declares Him to be one and alone: none like Him.

Spinoza thus comes to the basic conception of the one Universe, of "The All," maintained by the ancient Greeks, and which included both matter and mind, extension and thought. But this Universe, this "All," though identified by Spinoza with God in the light of revealed religion, is only the world of creation. Beyond it is the Creator, whose Primal Purpose, according to the Bab, creates, sustains, permits death, and then resuscitates. He is one and alone, because without Him nothing can be created, sustained, die and be reborn. None shares the absoluteness of His being, neither the physical universe, nor the human soul, neither matter nor mind. In short, the category of unity specifically pertains to God's creative Purpose which sustains all things.

41. AN EMPIRICAL APPROACH TO THE PANTHEISM OF SPINOZA

To follow a strictly mathematical method, and have every proposition follow necessarily from hypothetical premises in the form of initial definitions, renders a deductive reasoning at best, a flawless method of procedure. But that process alone does not establish objective truth, valid and positive, such as the spiritual and cultural life of man demands. Once these conclusions are attained, then the process of verification should start. It is this process of verification that finally established whether the premises and definitions were sound and objective. That such a process of verification is admitted in revealed religion, as valid and justified, is borne out by the saying of Jesus when he said: "By their fruits ye shall know them" (24). In other words, he made recognition of the claim to prophethood, which is the supreme problem of the religious life, subject to empirical verification. The same principle was uttered by Mohammed in the Koran when he said: "Observe, do you discover any flaw" (25), meaning in God's creation. The empirical method of reasoning and verification thus constituted a justified system of procedure, for ascertaining truth, both to Jesus and to Mohammed, but only as complementary to the deductive process, based upon premises revealed as Wisdom by God.

In his definitions and axioms, Spinoza tries to establish the doctrine of emanation as the major premise of all his thought. He includes under it the divine reality revealed in the prophets, as well as the human soul, considered as "thought," and physical objects of nature as "body." From this hypothetical premise, he then deduces his propositions. With these corollaries of Proposition 14, the practical implications of his premises start to make their appearance. Now can the validity of these conclusions be substantiated through the empirical process of verification? Does that method of reasoning, which is correct as far as the process of deduction goes, truly illumine our empirical discoveries, and establish the truth of different aspects of the spiritual and cultural life, initially derived through revelation? Putting the Spirit of Christ, that is, the Primal Purpose which animates all the prophets, together with the human soul, which is essentially spiritual in reality, and also a piece of stone, all as constituting the same divine substance—does such a premise give adequate explanation and value to the spiritual and cultural life of man, which is his supreme objective on earth?

In such a process of verification, it is not the careful mathematical method of Spinoza that is being questioned. That may be granted as sound. It is his basic definitions and major premises he endorses and accepts as a priori hypotheses that are being contested, and subjected to verification. For, as we have tried to show, parallel to the reasoning of Spinoza, and in contrast to it, we can put that of revealed religion, which is similarly deductive, and equally logical and correct; but based upon a different premise, namely, the Bab's dictum that there is no God but God, the Creator, and all else beside Him is His creation. Further that the principle of emanation applies exclusively to the divine nature revealed in the prophets; that the human soul, and objects of physical nature are merely "made," or "improved," by Him—in the Bab's language, created, sustained, left to languish and then resuscitated; that these are not an "overflow," or "radiation," from the Sun of the divine substance. Now, which of these two systems of thought, can best vindicate its premises through the empirical process of verification in the field of the spiritual and cultural life of man?

42. THE SYSTEM OF SPINOZA LEAVES NO GROUND FOR DISTINCTION BETWEEN THE CREATOR AND THE CREATED, OR BETWEEN THE REALITY OF THE VIRTUOUS AND THE NON-VIRTUOUS

If the creative process is an eternal, and constantly progressive, one; and substantiality is of the individual, undergoing that creative process; then we are bound to admit gradation of substantiality and reality to that entity. Put in the words of the Bab, there would be marked difference between the soul which has languished and "died," and that which has been given "life," and regenerated, by pursuing God's Primary Purpose, revealed by the prophets. Under the doctrine of emanation, there would be no ground for either substantial or formal difference between the two; the difference between the virtuous and the non-virtuous would be merely a matter of consciousness of an existing unity of substance. Nor would there be ground for substantial difference between the Creator and the created. Both these cases are brought out by Baha'u'llah when he says: "Let no one imagine that by our assertion that all created things are signs of the revelation of God is meant that—God forbid—all men, be they good or evil, pious or infidel, are equal in the sight of God. Nor doth it imply that the divine Being—magnified be His name and exalted be His glory—is under any circumstance comparable unto men, or can, in any way, be associated with His creatures. Such an error hath been committed by certain foolish ones who, after having ascended into the heavens of their idle fancies, have interpreted Divine Unity to mean that all created things are the signs of God, and that, consequently, there is no distinction whatever between them. Some have even outstripped them by maintaining that these signs are peers and partners of God Himself. Gracious God! He, verily, is one in His essence, one in His attributes. Everything besides Him is as nothing when brought face to face with the resplendent revelation of but one of His names, with no more than the faintest intimation of His glory—how much less when confronted with His own self! . . . . Say: O people! How can a fleeting fancy compare with the Self-Subsisting, and how can the Creator be likened unto His creatures, who are but as the script of His pen? Nay, His script excelleth all things, and is sanctified from, and immeasurably exalted above, all creatures" (26).

By the reference here made to those who fail to distinguish between the virtuous and the wicked, the faithful followers of the prophets, who have

110

been regenerated by the Primal Purpose, and the infidels who have not, by these is meant some schools of mystics who try to transcend religion, its dictates and the substantial gradation and reality it attributes to individual human souls on the ground that they are all in substance one with God. These maintain that religion is for the uninitiated, for the ignorant, who is not already awakened to the fact that he is in substance and essence one with God; that there is no difference between the prophets and the individual man, save that they have been made conscious of that truth and fact, while the latter have not. Both have the divine element or "sign" within them, the one potentially, the other in full actuality.

Nothing can better express the genius of a painter than his painting or reveal the creative power and imagination of an artisan fuller than his artifact. Not only his genius, but also his purpose, ideas, sentiments and ends, all are revealed there. Similarly, nothing can better unfold the creative power of God, His Primary Purpose, His love for man, the ends He tries to realize on earth, than the creation of the physical universe, and the generation, sustenance, death and life of humanity and its spiritual and cultural being. As Baha'u'llah says, these are "signs" that reveal the power and Purpose of God, and the love he entertains for man. But it is a flagrant error to maintain that this painting, this artifact, the physical creation, or the spiritual reality of man, can be likened to its creator, much less to be substantially identified with Him. This is why Jesus said: "Ye are from beneath; I am from above: ye are of this world; I am not of this world"(27). The spiritual reality in man cannot be compared with the divine nature revealed in Jesus; how much less can physical nature be identified with the Father. The divine nature revealed in the prophets is an emanation of God; the human soul and physical being are merely His handiwork, and "signs" or traces of His creative power, and Primal Purpose, throughout the universe.

To put it in the terminology of the Bayan, if the human soul is like a mirror, reflecting the light of God, which proceeds from the prophets, and through that illumination is created, sustained, perishes, and is revived, and regenerated, into an ever higher stage of being; then how can we identify the being, and substantiality, of this created soul, with the reality of the prophets as its creator? Even though the human soul evolves, and gradually advances on the way to perfection, to full reflection of the divine attributes; yet it is a created reality, a mirror, fully dependent upon the prophets for its light: its creation, sustenance, death, and spiritual and cultural rebirth (28). Though there are gradations of being, and levels of substantiality through which the human soul evolves, yet, according to the Bab, they have limits that it cannot trespass. It cannot transcend its nature as created, as a mirror receiving its light, and illumination, from the prophets of God. For, as the Bab says, the sea of the world of creation cannot be identified with, or merge into, the ocean of divine Being.

43. BAHA'U'LLAH ON THE UNITY OF GOD'S ESSENCE AND ATTRIBUTES

Baha'u'llah says that, God "is one in His Essence, one in His attributes," because the essence and attributes of His creatures are absolutely different from His. Physical nature and thought, are not attributes of divine Being. God is a simple reality and, as such, transcends all attributes we ascribe to Him. As we have observed, these attributes apply solely to His Primal Purpose, His revelation, to His prophets who, like mirrors, or prisms, break up that simple reality, or light, into its different hues. It is the action of the prism that is the source of the plurality of those colors and shades. It is the acts performed by the prophets, in the different environments, and fields of individual and social interests, which they share with man, that is the cause of the plurality of the attributes we term divine. Intellect, or mind, is one such attribute. How can we, therefore, ascribe it to God, Who is of a simple, and transcendent, reality? How can we identify "extension," and hence physical nature, which is subject to time and space, with God Who transcends them both?

"As to those sayings, attributed to the Prophets of old," Baha'u'llah says, "such as 'In the beginning was God; there was no creature to know Him,' and 'The Lord was alone; with no one to adore Him,' the meaning of these and similar sayings is clear and evident, and should at no time be misapprehended. To this same truth bear witness these words which He hath revealed: 'God was alone; there was none else besides Him. He will always remain what He hath ever been.' Every discerning eye will readily perceive that the Lord is now manifest, yet there is none to recognize His glory. By this is meant that the habitation wherein the Divine Being dwelleth is far above the reach and ken of any one besides Him. Whatsoever in the contingent world can either be expressed or apprehended can never transgress the limits which by its inherent nature have been imposed upon it. God, alone, transcendeth such limitations. He, verily, is from everlasting. No peer or partner has been, or can ever be, joined with Him. No name can be compared with His Name. No pen can portray His nature, neither can any tongue depict His glory. He will, for ever, remain immeasurably exalted above any one except Himself.

"Consider the hour at which the supreme Manifestation of God revealeth Himself unto men. Ere that hour cometh, the Ancient Being, Who is still unknown of men and hath not as yet given utterance to the Word of God, is Himself the All-Knower in a world devoid of any man that hath known Him. He is indeed the Creator without a creation. For at the very moment preceding His Revelation, each and every created thing shall be made to yield up its soul to God. This is indeed the Day of which it hath been written: 'Whose shall be the Kingdom this Day?' And none can be found ready to answer!"(29)

44. THE RESULTS OF PANTHEISM IN THE FIELD OF CULTURE

The consequence of Pantheism, of identifying God with physical nature, is far-reaching in the field of culture and the spiritual life of man. It does not remain as an abstract theory, but is apt to affect the cultural evolution of society. Man is born in the lap of nature, and on the level with animal life. His spiritual and cultural values and progress he acquires to the extent he transcends that nature. As part of the world of creation, and its process of becoming, he is, as the Bab would express it, subject to "death"; for he is always apt to fall back to the level of nature, if the Creator does not "sustain" him, and impart to him a new "life." This inveterate tendency, to fall back to the level of nature, is best observed in his drift towards naturalism, and identifying God with nature, whenever revealed religion loosens its grasp on human consciousness, and fails to inspire and guide man.

To consider everything, both objects of nature and the human soul, "signs," or traces, of the infinite creative power of God, is to impart to them a spiritual value and significance. It is to observe in them the fruits of His infinite love and universal dominion and sovereignty, as well as the capacity of "all other than Him" to reflect ever more fully, His attributes of perfection as they progress to higher levels of being. Everything will tell of His Primal Purpose but none will be likened to Him. He will be in His exalted station, as creater, "one and alone."

If, however, we identify God's substance and essence with nature and

113

the individual human soul instead of raising the level of these, we lower the station of God. We make Him subject to physical categories of being, subject to time and space, which are too empirically and positively real, to be denied or overlooked; we subject His nature to the pluralism, manifest in the world of nature, and make it the basis of the personality and individuality of the human soul. And that constitutes the heathenism, from which revealed religion has, down the ages, tried to deliver mankind.

45. BASIS OF CONTRAST BETWEEN REVEALED RELIGION AND PAGAN THOUGHT

The distinctive feature of revealed religion, when contrasted with pagan systems of thought, is that its reasoning is based upon two major premises: (a) that, God is an absolutely transcendent reality; (b) that the sole means whereby man can attain a knowledge of the divine will and purpose, as well as formulate a conception of His attributes of perfection which, he has gradually to acquire, is through His successive revelations. This insertion of the divine nature of the prophets as self-revelation of a transcendent God thus distinguishes the system of thought of revealed religion from all others, including Idealism, Empiricism, and Mysticism: all of which have their roots deep in ancient pagan conceptions. And when the absolute transcendence of God to both the human soul and physical nature is discarded the result is that religion, as source of the spiritual and cultural life, falls back to the level of nature, and becomes itself naturalistic in trend and purpose.

Idealism stresses that mind is "separate," that it dominates the physical senses, and belongs to a realm of being far beyond that of matter. But it fails to consider God as absolutely transcendent to mind. It rather tends to identify God with the principle of intellection, as universal Reason. While reason, or mind, is a mere faculty of man, upon this level of his existence. For this reason Greek Idealism becomes naturalistic in tendency. Thus, even though mind is considered "separate," and beyond the realm of physical being, yet, because God is identified with it, and it is itself a faculty of man, He is pulled down to the level of the human soul, and reduced to the principle of order within nature. God is not considered as the transcendent efficient Cause, and Creator, of the very being of nature, as but the rational law which pervades it, and gives it order.

114

Empiricism, which is also rooted in pagan conceptions, is even more naturalistic in tendency: for it identifies Reality with natural phenomena, and considers the human soul, or "thought," as a product of sense-perception, devoid of any spiritual substance, beyond the province of nature. In other words, it considers God as Universal Reason permeating physical nature, rather than "separate" from it.

Even mysticism is not free from this naturalistic tendency, though it disparages physical existence, and claims to sever man's relation from it, but its naturalistic tendencies are not less pronounced than those of Rationalism which it generally denounces. For, instead of mind, it takes another natural faculty of man, namely, emotion or intuition, and according to the principle that only "like can know its like," and feel one with it, identifies the human soul with the substance of God. But, by being identified with the human soul, God is drawn to the level of nature, and identified with it as well. This is the reason why mysticism ends by being Pantheistic. And when the creative force which ought to undertake the upliftment of man, and the constant regeneration of his spiritual and cultural life, is made naturalistic, and brought down to the level of nature, then no upliftment can be effected. Creation as "improvement," ceases to have significance, and salvation as entering into a higher stage of being becomes devoid of meaning. The final outcome is that cultural life remains natural in origin, and the purpose of human endeavour is to revert to the level of nature. The moral life thus remains the satisfaction of natural instincts; justice continues to be interpreted as the rule of the strong, and the law of the jungle; and beauty considered in terms of physical forms. In short, by being pantheistic and hence naturalistic in tendency mysticism cannot transcend nature and rid itself from a naturalistic interpretation of the higher values.

46. PANTHEISM TENDS TO MAKE RELIGION NATURALISTIC

This change in the conception of God, from absolute transcendence to immanence and naturalism, has far-reaching spiritual and cultural consequences. And in Pantheism, which is its extreme form, it becomes most vivid. And the field in which these results are best expressed is that of religion. No matter what our attitude towards the spiritual life may be, religion is a historical phenomenon, which has exerted considerable influence upon human life and activity from time immemorial; and its basic tenets have provided thought with its major premises. The nature of the origins of religion, therefore, constitutes an outstanding issue for man: a problem he has to confront and solve.

Religion as revelation from God, vouchsafed through the medium of Jesus Christ, was fast losing ground in the sixteenth and seventeenth centuries because of the inadequate way it was represented, and practiced, and taught by the Church to an intellectually awakened and alert people in Europe. The transcendence of God was being gradually discarded through the doctrine of universal emanation; and the principle that Jesus Christ was the intermediary, acting as a channel for the revelation of the divine will and purpose, was being set aside. With these two basic premises of revealed religion discarded, thought began to recede to naturalistic tendencies. The natural consequence was a reversion to ancient Greek Idealism, Empiricism and Mysticism, and their respective interpretation of the spiritual life, all of which tried to side-step the principle of prophethood as necessary medium of revelation. On the ground that God is immanent in thought, Rationalism and Idealism maintained that intellect, or the human conscience, is the source from which the voice of God is heard, and, therefore, religious values spring. But considered in that light, religion becomes an intellectual approach, a priori in method, for interpreting the phenomena of nature.

Empiricists considered God to be immanent, not only in human thought, but also in physical nature. Hence, the spiritual experience of man was to detect His presence, and accordingly find the origins of religion in nature itself. It was due to such metaphysical principles that the religion of primitive peoples was studied, and interpreted as fetishism, sorcery, totemism and animism. It was similarly a recession to the level of naturalism which revived interest in ancient mysticism, and stimulated its development and spread.

All these interpretations of the source of religion, or the spiritual life, grew to prominence as a direct result of discarding the conception of an absolutely transcendent God, revealing Himself periodically through the medium of His successive prophets. All these were interpretations, substantially naturalistic, for the origin of religion, and the spiritual life. They were all recessions from the principle of revealed religion. For according to this latter, revelation is the only source of religion. It is the spiritual and cultural rebirth of mankind, effected through the revelation of God's Primal Purpose. Fetishism, sorcery, animism, totemism and the

116

like are man-made accretions added to it by primitive imagination and it is the supreme task of revealed religion to free itself from them, and from the distortions of truth they represent.

47. SPINOZA'S NATURALISM: "Whatever is," says Spinoza, "is in God, and nothing can exist or be conceived without God" (Prop. XV). There are three points to be considered in connection with this proposition: (a) that the expression "in" subjects God to the category of space; (b) that, all things "exist" through God; (c) that, all things are "conceived" through Him.

In his note to this proposition Spinoza defines "body" as "a certain quantity in length, breadth, and depth with a certain shape." Though he states that this definition is given by his adversaries, he seems to endorse it; for he admits that his monism, and the unity of substance he maintains, renders physical being an attribute of God. "Hence, we conclude," he says, "that extended substance is one of the infinite attributes of God." But he attempts to show that the objection levelled against him, by those who maintain the principle of creation, that is, followers of revealed religion, is wrong; for it separates the corporeal, or extended substance, from the divine nature; and in such a case, we are justified to ask, "From what divine power it could have been created"?

This argument of Spinoza is applicable, not to creation as "improvement," as impressing a new and higher form, upon an existing individual reality, to raise it to a higher stage of being, as revealed religion maintains. It applies to a misinterpreted and misunderstood conception of creation which, we have observed, contradicts the eternity, and everlastingness, of God's creative power and Purpose. Creation out of an absolute "void" was a problem confronting Greek philosophy, because it was a tenet of ancient heathenism, which it tried to combat. To the prophets, creation has always been giving form to the formless, and therefore, a higher stage of being both in physical nature, and in the spiritual and cultural life of man. And that process has been operating eternally in the past, and will everlastingly in the future, constantly and unceasingly. In other words, the aversion of Spinoza was to a conception of creation wrongly attributed to revealed religion and imbedded in ancient heathenism which had permeated contemporary Christian thought, and became a philosophic view.

117

48. THE SUPER-NATURALISM OF REVEALED RELIGION

The fundamental dictum of the Bab that all other than God is His creation constitutes the basis of this religious supernaturalism, for it establishes the principle that this "all else" is not an emanation of God, and hence substantially one with Him; but rather, that it is His handiwork and artifact. Furthermore, the principle of gradation of being, which revealed religion maintains, and the fact that physical nature constitutes the lowest grade on which man is born make the spiritual and cultural evolution of man supernatural in its goal. For it projects that progress and growth into stages of being far above the physical and the natural plane. And the human soul can proceed beyond that plane because, as a spiritual reality, it belongs to a higher stage of existence. Categories of understanding applicable to physical nature cannot be rightly applied to it. As Baha'u'llah says: "The human soul is exalted above all egress and regress"(30); that is, special considerations. And if the human soul, because it is a spiritual entity, transcends special considerations, how much more is the spirit of God, which is the creator of all things, both spiritual and material. In other words, categories of being which apply to the physical are inapplicable to a reality that is essentially spiritual, and characteristics that are essentially of the created cannot be attributed to the Creator. Time and space are concomitants of the contingent and of the physical; hence they cannot apply to the purely spiritual or "unmoved" and changeless. They are attributes of the created, not of the absolute. It is true that they possess positive reality, a reality which is as positive as the created objects themselves, but they apply only to these. The human soul, being in nature and substance spirit, transcends space; but being subject to a process of development, and of acquiring perfections, it is subject to time in its gradual growth. God is a reality which besides being spiritual is an unmoved Mover. As a spiritual reality He transcends space; as unmoved Mover He transcends time. These categories, therefore, do not apply to Him; hence "extension" cannot be one of His attributes. And it is in that sense that He is considered "infinite." All limitations of time and space are inapplicable to His divine substance. Even "thought" is subject to definition, and therefore is inapplicable to Him.

49. IDEAS, OR "THOUGHT," TRANSCEND TIME AND SPACE, AND YET ARE NOT IDENTICAL WITH GOD, FOR THEY ARE CREATED

Because Ideas are abstract, universal, rational entities, they are neither corporal, and "extended," nor subject to change, once formulated, and hence to time. And on that ground, they are usually regarded as infinite and eternal. It was on such a ground that ancient thought identified the idea of the Good with God. Both God and Ideas, or Forms, are eternal, unchanging and infinite; and hence were apt to be identified; but was that identification justified? It does not mean that because God is infinite and eternal He transcends the categories of time and space, that, on that ground, He is an Idea or Form. An Idea is a universal that possesses a mere rational and intellectual existence. It is a mere essence, a definition. It is an abstraction with inchoate substantial existence. It has no positive, objective being, independent of a mind to conceive it. While God is a substantial being, with no knowable essence, utterly unaffected whether known or not. He is not an intellectual abstraction, a mere rational conception in some mind. As creator He defines, and is not a definition, as an idea is. And these distinctions are foundational; otherwise we may fall into the error of considering God as a conception man has devised to interpret the incomprehensible phenomena of nature, in other words, a mere hypothesis of human thought.

Time and space are concomitants of creation. Eternity and infinity merely denote transcendence to them; when there is neither a creative process involving time, nor corporality implying space. Eternity means inapplicability of the category of time to a reality which is changeless; whether that reality be a substantial "unmoved Mover," or an intellectual abstraction, or definition, which by its very nature is changeless and formal. Infinity means that the defining lines or dimensions, applicable to corporal things, are transcended, that they do not apply to a reality which is essentially spiritual. In other words, eternity and infinity are, like other attributes given by man to God, essentially negative in nature. They deny the possibility of limiting and defining, which are characteristics of created objects. These, that is, infinity and eternity, are not positive attributes, and objective characteristics; therefore, how can we identify God with Idea and Form, on the ground that they are all infinite and eternal? There is an equivocation in the two terms which we should not overlook. Infinity and eternity, when applied to Ideas and Forms, denote

119

a universal definition and nature; when applied to God, they imply inapplicability of limiting lines, and definition. And if eternity and infinity imply totally different characteristics when applied to Ideas, on the one hand, and to God, on the other; how can we say with Spinoza that they have unity of attributes, and therefore are in substance the same?

50. THE INDIVIDUAL BOTH CREATES AND IS THE PRODUCT OF CREATION

Spinoza tries to refute the principle of creation on the ground that one substance cannot produce another, according to Prop. 6. This may be true, but only if we define substance formally as Rationalism does, that is, if we identify it with Idea or Form. The principle may be made to apply within the rationalistic system of thought, as conclusion to its specific premises. A universal, changeless, abstract conception cannot produce another conception also universal and abstract, and yet be considered substantially different. For both would be Idea or Form, and hence substantially the same, by the very definition they presume. "For substance" as Spinoza says, "can neither be made nor destroyed."

Revealed religion, however, does not uphold that rationalistic interpretation or definition of substance. Its doctrine of creation involves the principle that both the creator and the product of His creation are individual realities. Pure form and pure matter, are intellectual abstractions of positive reality. Substantial existence pertains to the individual, either as creator or as created. Nature teems with signs, or traces, showing the revelation of what Spinoza calls "divine power," acting as the cause of the integration of individual things into ever higher entities. The spiritual and cultural life is of individual men, and effected by individual prophets, who have appeared down the centuries. In other words, if we attribute substantial reality to the individual, then creation as integration, and improvement, becomes the most "clear and distinct" phenomenon we observe, not only in the physical universe, but also in the spiritual and cultural life of man, with the individual prophets standing as the creators.

51. THE UNITY OF THE SPIRITUAL AND CULTURAL LIFE IS DUE TO THE UNITY OF THE PRIMAL PURPOSE WHICH ANIMATES THE INDIVIDUAL PROPHETS

But does the plurality of the prophets, or creators of the spiritual and cultural life, and the plurality of the created individual human beings impair the unity of the universe, which philosophy down the ages has tried to visualize? Ancient Greek thought sought that unity in substance, whether that substance was formal, such as maintained by Plato, or material, such as advocated by Heracleitus. In contrast to both these schools of thought, revealed religion based the unity of the universe upon the unity of the Primal Purpose, which pervades and dominates all the world of creation and is revealed in the divine nature of the prophets. Such a unity, instead of abstracting substantial reality from the individual, and setting it apart in an idea, or in matter, maintains it in the individual as the supremely and concretely real, the fruit and product of God's creative Purpose, revealed by the individual prophets.

52. SPINOZA CONSIDERS TIME AND SPACE AS MODES OF GOD

In trying to prove the substantial unity of God and nature, Spinoza had maintained that they are both infinite; and being infinite, and hence identical in attribute, he reasoned, they were substantially the same. For no two entities can have the same attributes and be different in substance. In his note to the proposition, Spinoza returns to that argument for further elucidation. He starts by referring to the anthropomorphic conception of God, held by some, and sets it aside as too untenable to be worthy of consideration. Then he admits that "body," which is subject to dimensions, cannot be identified with God Who is infinite, and hence beyond them. But such freedom from physical dimensions, he says, does not justify us to separate completely between God and the corporeal or extended. For, he says, there is no "power" which can account for this creation or its generation. Then he concludes that, though corporeal objects, which are subject to the three dimensions, cannot be identified with God, they are nevertheless attributes of the divine nature, and in substance one with Him. In other words, that dimensions are categories applicable to the "modes" of God, though not to His own being; that though corporality is characteristic of the divine attribute, namely, "body," it is not of the divine substance itself. And to prove this, he reverts to the question of infinity, "for all these arguments," he says, "seem to return to this point," namely, that "in the first place, that corporeal substance, as far as it is substance, consists, they think, of parts: consequently they deny that it can be infinite and consequently appertain to God." In other words, he says that the advocates of the doctrine of creation do not believe in the infinite divisibility of substance which is corporeal, hence in its infinity—the attribute predicated of God. The absurdity of the advocates of the principle of creation, he says, is in this, "that they suppose an infinite quantity to be measurable and composed of infinite parts," while "an infinite quantity is not measurable nor composed of finite parts." "And indeed it is no less absurd to suppose that corporeal substance is composed of bodies or parts than to suppose that a body is composed of surfaces, or surfaces of lines, and lines of points."

53. THE TERM "INFINITY" IS EQUIVOCAL

Spinoza admits that God transcends corporeality, in the sense that the dimensions which define the latter are inapplicable to His nature. In that sense God is considered "infinite." In a similar sense would a plane transcend depth, or a line width, or a point all dimensions. There are infinite points in a line because of that transcendence: because it has no length. And on that ground a line cannot be divided into points, or a plane into lines. The basic categories of their being differ. On the other hand, we might say that a line can be projected to infinity. In this case the extension would be better defined as "indefinitely" for the dimension in question would not be transcended, but maintained all through. Similarly, physical or corporeal nature can be divided, or extended to "infinity" or "indefinitely" because it can be projected without transcending those specific dimensions, because no point can be designated when that specific dimension can be considered as ended and exhausted. All special extensions of physical nature, therefore, can be "indefinitely" projected with this reservation that at any point within that dimension there is the possibility of setting a limit, and considering that magnitude so limited, a definite entity, with a specific action and reaction, or relation, with other entities. Thus, the indefinitely extended universe may be divided into galaxies, these into solar systems, these latter into astral bodies, and so on down the scale until, we reach electrons, and perhaps beyond. All these remain subject to the special dimension of length, breadth and volume, with the possibility of stopping at some specific limits, and considering that magnitude as constituting an entity, acting and reacting with its environment as an individual being. But at no time can we transcend those dimensions, unless the entity is purely rational and abstract idea, such as a point, and thereby denies its corporeality.

54. THE HUMAN SOUL, BEING SPIRITUAL, TRANSCENDS CORPOREAL DIMENSIONS; BUT BEING CREATED, HAD A BEGINNING IN TIME, AND BEING SUBJECT TO A PROCESS OF EVOLUTION, IS SUBJECT TO TEMPORAL PROGRESSION

The human soul, being spiritual in substance, completely transcends corporeal dimensions and categories of being. Such a spiritual reality cannot be divided "indefinitely," nor extended "indefinitely"; for neither of these special considerations are applicable to its nature. But being created, the human soul has a beginning in time, and being subject to a process of evolution and growth, it is subject to the progress of time. Thus, though it is "spaceless," it is not "timeless." It is created, sustained, left to perish, and then resuscitated, in time.

Such being the case, how can we confuse the "indefinite" possibility of extension, peculiar to "body," and physical nature, with the "spacelessness" of a spiritual reality? Similarly, how can we confuse the human soul, which has a beginning, and is subject to progression, in time with the substance of God which is absolutely beyond spacial and temporal considerations? And after assuming such untenable premises assert that, having the same attribute of "infinity," they are all in substance the same? There is an equivocation of the term "infinity" which we have to take into account, otherwise all our reasoning will be false.

55. PASSIVITY OF CREATED OBJECTS CANNOT BE CONFUSED WITH PURE ACTIVITY OF THE CREATOR

After dealing with the controversy centered around the divisibility of "body" into parts Spinoza takes up the one based upon the idea that physical being is passive, and hence, cannot be identified with God's substance which, as "unmoved Mover," is fully active. We have already dealt with this point, and quoted Baha'u'llah questioning the validity of any reasoning which attempts to identify the substance of a painter with that of his handiwork. We cannot identify the reality of the divine element, revealed in the prophets, which manifests all of God's attributes of perfection in full actuality and which acts as channel of His creative Primal Purpose, with the human soul which is mere capacity and receptivity. The one, like the sun, radiates light; the other, like a mirror, merely receives and reflects it. The one imparts the ideas and forms through which human regeneration is achieved; the other merely submits himself to that process, and is thereby evolved. The spiritual and cultural purpose man has to make his own, the intellectual, moral, social and aesthetic perfections he has to acquire, and the destiny he has to seek and strive to attain, all are proffered to him by the prophets. Without their guidance his life is devoid of purpose, value and significance. How can we, therefore, identify the nature and substance of the two?

56. PARTICIPATION IN GOD'S CREATIVE PURPOSE IS THE FUNCTION ACQUIRED BY MAN

Similarly, once the human soul has learned the purpose of its life and being upon this earth, and obtained a clear vision and understanding of the attributes of perfection, revealed by the prophets: the Ideas and Forms it has to acquire, and gradually make its own, then it becomes itself a positive force, with a purpose, aim, and ideas in line with the divine will. Man then becomes active to the extent he has merged his will in God's creative purpose. Having attained that state, he will not wait passively to receive impressions made on its senses, to be moved and to react. His mind will not be that of a mere "observer," and play the role of a plate of wax, ready to receive impressions from outside. He becomes a dynamic force with a creative mission to fulfil. When he attains such a state of dedication to the divine Cause, his intellect and physical senses become instruments to serve a supreme purpose. Once the human soul falls in line with God's creative purpose, it becomes active and positive; and the forces of nature passive in respect to it. He starts to impress values he has acquired upon the cultural environment he lives in and recasts it accordingly. As such, man becomes the potter, and the intellectual, moral, social, and aesthetic life of society, the clay at his disposal. Physical nature becomes pure passivity, before the dominating cultural purpose of man. And if that be true, how can we identify the two, namely, the human soul and physical nature, in substance and reality? Their action and reaction, their functions, properties and attributes will bear witness that they belong to different strata of being. The one will have the substance of a creator, the other of a created.

57. GOD AS THE RATIONAL CAUSE OF ALL THINGS

"Infinite things," Spinoza says, "in infinite modes (that is, all things which can fall under the heading of infinite intellect) must necessarily follow from the necessity of divine nature" (Prop. 16). This proposition deals with God as universal Reason, and rational Cause of all things;

which is brought out more fully in the three following corollaries: (a) "Hence it follows that God is the effecting cause of all things which can be perceived by infinite intellect; (b) hence it follows that God is the cause through himself, and not indeed by accident; (c) hence it follows that God is absolutely the first cause."

Two principles are involved in this proposition: first, that ultimate reality is in the nature of Mind, or universal Reason; secondly, that all things flow out of it as "modes," retaining thereby the unity of their intellectual substance. In his proof, Spinoza starts by maintaining that from a given definition intellect gathers certain properties, which it considers the essence of that thing. Furthermore, the more reality an object possesses, the more the intellect can discern properties and include them in the definition. As the divine nature is an infinite reality and possesses infinite characteristics, infinite attributes necessarily flow out of His nature. In other words, God is considered here both as the supreme intellectual reality, or universal Mind, and also as the supreme object of understanding. He is regarded as the highest object of human knowledge, because He possesses definable essence and characteristics.

58. TO CONSIDER GOD AS "INFINITE INTELLECT" IS ANTHROPOMORPHIC

There are two alternative ways revealed religion can confront this proposition of Spinoza. To say that God, or ultimate Reality, is in the nature of Mind or intellect leads, according to revealed religion, to anthropomorphism, for which Spinoza himself expresses disavowal. To consider God as mind, or principle of intellection, is tantamount to considering Him with human form and physical features. For mind is just as much a human faculty as any of the others are. And the position does not alter by terming it "infinite." In fact, God is "spirit," as Jesus said, in the sense that He is not intelligible, not an object of human understanding, and hence, undefinable. As the Bab said, God's essence is far beyond human knowledge and His essence comprises His inherent characteristics. And if this premise be admitted, then all subsequent reasoning lose their validity.

59. "INFINITE INTELLECT" CONSTITUTES "WISDOM" REVEALED BY THE PROPHETS

Absolute transcendence of the divine Essence to human thought leads us to the second alternative, namely, that "infinite Intellect" can apply

125

only to "Wisdom" revealed by the prophets. In that case, rationalism which seeks a God Who is the principle of intellection, and its source, will have to reconcile itself with revealed religion, and regard the supreme reality, knowable to man, not the Godhead, or the divine Essence, but His revelation as the source of "Wisdom." Only thus can rationalism obtain a significance empirically and historically verifiable. In other words, the supreme reality rationalism seeks is the revelation of God as "Wisdom," within the sphere of man's possible understanding. Hence the Idea of the Good, which to Plato was the supreme object of understanding and the source of all illumination, and the Form of all forms which to Aristotle constituted both the supreme Knower, and the highest object of knowledge both apply to the divine nature revealed in the prophets, and that as a positive historical and verifiable fact. In other words, in the divine nature revealed in the prophets, the highest object of understanding and the principle and source of all intellection join; similarly, the source of all goodness and the Good towards which all moral and ethical life tends as the supreme objective. Likewise it constitutes the supreme form of beauty, and the highest object of the aesthetic life of man. In short, in the divine nature of the prophets centers the efficient, final, and formal cause of man's spiritual and cultural life. Referring to that divine nature revealed in the prophets, Baha'u'llah says: "The first station, which is related to His (the prophet's) innermost reality, representeth Him as One Whose voice is the voice of God Himself. To this testifieth the tradition (from Mohammed). . . . Arise, O Mohammed, for lo, the Lover and the Beloved are joined together and made one in Thee"(31). Therefore, the value of all things, and hence, their nature as affecting human weal, "must necessarily follow from the necessity of the divine nature," only if by "divine nature" be meant that which is revealed in the prophets.

60. THE PRINCIPLE OF FREEDOM

"God," says Spinoza, "acts merely according to his own laws, and is compelled by no one" (Prop. XVII). If all things are "modes" of the divine substance, flowing out of His nature in the form of attributes, if there is nothing other than, and beyond, that divine nature, then all things act and move according to it. Nothing would exist outside the divine nature to determine its activities and influence its laws. "Hence it follows that no cause can be given except the perfection of God's nature which extrinsically or intrinsically incites him to action'' (Cor. 1).

In his note appended to this proposition, Spinoza starts by considering the type of freedom which implies ability to perform things contradictory to the very nature of their being, such as to construct a triangle the sum of whose angles is not equal to two right angles. But that is not the type of freedom revealed religion, with its doctrine of creation, attributes to God. Spinoza maintains that ''nothing outside God can exist by which he could be determined or compelled in his actions.'' How can we interpret this statement in the light of the doctrine of creation maintained by revealed religion?

61. THE FREE IN THE SENSE OF THE UNDETERMINED AND UNDEFINABLE

The first point to stress is that freedom, like any other attribute of perfection, cannot be predicated of the divine Essence without being involved in anthropomorphism. The principle of freedom of choice is fundamental for the spiritual and cultural life of man; and it is in that field that we have to detect it as an objective intelligible reality. To attribute it to God, or the transcendent divine Essence, is to picture Him in human image, and attribute to Him characteristics which man ought to possess to achieve spiritual and moral perfection. Hence, freedom like all other attributes of perfection, to bear value, significance, and objective validity, should be referred not to the transcendent divine Essence, but to the divine nature revealed in the prophets, and manifested in their creative purpose and activity. In other words, it is in the divine nature revealed in the prophets that we have to seek for the principle of freedom, which is the ground of moral choice and cultural development of man. Only in a negative sense can we predicate freedom to God, the transcendent Essence. He is free in the sense that He is undetermined, and hence undefined. For to define is to state the limits, to determine is to set the limiting lines; and that implies creation and generation. God is free in the sense that He is the creator of all things, and therefore unencumbered by definition and limitations. He sets the limits to the world of creation, and thereby determines its nature, purpose and course, but Himself transcends those limits. He is free from all determining lines. Only in such a negative sense can we attribute freedom to God.

127

62. FREEDOM AND THE PRINCIPLE OF EMANATION

If proceeding from God were confined to emanation, that is, if "infinite things in infinite modes," that is, all things necessarily flow, or overflow from God's nature and being as waves that surge from the sea, or rays of light radiate from the sun; then nothing would exist other than His divine nature to "determine" the manner of His activity, or the nature of His laws, and the ground of His values. It would be like the projection of a point in empty space with nothing to deflect its course or deviate its direction. The only determining force would be the one inherent in itself. This principle is fully applicable to the divine nature revealed in the prophets for the human nature these possess is fully dedicated to their mission. They act like a flute, empty from their physical self and individual desires, and therefore give full vent to God as the player to breathe His tune. And that principle is true to them, because their divine nature is a "flow" from and a projection of God's being and nature. But this principle of determinism does not apply to the world of creation, especially to the spiritual and cultural life of man where freedom is given by God a moral role to play.

63. FREEDOM AND THE PRINCIPLE OF CREATION

As we have already observed, the spiritual and cultural life of man is not absolutely determined according to a primordial necessity. For, this is the sphere of guidance rather than of necessity and compulsion. It is the field where man is left free by God Himself to follow his destiny, according to the primal Purpose revealed by the prophets, or to disregard it, and bear the consequences. Here freedom is not due to an inner law and necessity, not to the absence of external compulsion, but rather to the existence of a restricted sphere wherein God, as creator, has permitted man a measure of liberty to develop his own personality, and positively participate in the creation of his spiritual and cultural life. It is not an absence of an external determinant but a positive sphere and form of activity afforded to man as distinguished from all other created things.

This freedom given to man, as part of his spiritual and cultural environment, when employed in pursuit of the realization of God's creative Purpose leads to human salvation and the full growth of the

128

spiritual and cultural life, but when applied in defiance of that guidance leads inevitably to the deterioration of that life. And history presents ample evidence for the existence of such periods, when man's face is deliberately turned towards waywardness, and as a result, chaos and "formlessness" prevail.

64. THE APPEARANCE OF FREEDOM OF CHOICE, IN THE SPIRITUAL AND CULTURAL LIFE, IS DUE TO THE FACT THAT IT CONSTITUTES THE DOMAIN WHEREIN THE FORMAL CAUSE OPERATES

Whereas the "determining" cause, the defining factor in the world of creation generally, is the efficient cause, which moves by "compulsion"; in the specific, and restricted, sphere of the spiritual and cultural life, the creative force is the formal cause, what Jesus attributed to himself as "exemplary." This formal Cause, which operates through the prophets, does not move man by an inner or external compulsion, but by setting an ultimate goal and purpose for human evolution, and calling on man to strive and attain them. This formal Cause leaves to individual judgment, and desire, to be drawn to that supreme exemplary, and thereby acquire the perfections revealed; or to disregard them, and bear the evil consequences. That formal Cause is by its very nature, a transcendent force, and an object of human contemplation and understanding; but the influence it exerts cannot be termed "compulsion." It operates as a source of guidance, and an object of love and admiration. It merely calls on man to achieve perfection using his own understanding, independent deliberation, and free choice. In other words, in the sphere of the spiritual and cultural life, two elements present themselves to man, as part of the creative pursuit he undertakes; namely, (a) rational understanding and (b) free choice, of his purpose and the values he has thereby to adopt. And both of these are the direct consequences of the nature of the influence the prophets of God exert on human life. Acting as merely the formal Cause of human evolution, they do not operate as an external "compelling" force, driving man to perfection; but as a supreme object of understanding, contemplation and love, which merely calls man to his goal, giving him ample measure of individual deliberation and free choice.

65. THE DETERMINING FACTORS ARE NOT CONFINED TO THE REVELATION OF THE DIVINE NATURE, BUT ARE ALSO RELATIVE TO THE CONDITION OF THE CREATED

A disintegrated society, composed of spiritually depraved individuals, constitutes the "formless" clay the prophets as creators recast and remolded into a new being. Every such social and individual state of depravity, and formlessness, presents its own type of difficulties, its own specific and objective problems, to the creator just as every type of clay presents its own, to the potter or sculptor. The problems that confronted humanity, at the time of Jesus, or Mohammed, were not like those of today. It is the spiritual and cultural issues of their own specific age and dispensation which confront the prophets. The condition of the world and the stage of individual and social revolution at least partly determine the course the Primal Purpose has to pursue. At different stages of human evolution, the prophets confront different social and individual problems, which they have to take into consideration, in pursuing God's creative purpose on earth. Different laws and different social institutions are required to further the same eternal Purpose. In other words, in the field of creation, God's Purpose is not determined solely by the necessity of His own goal. It takes into consideration the constantly changing and evolving nature of man, and his spiritual and cultural level of growth, and defines values accordingly.

But such consideration of the needs of the spiritual and cultural life of man, such type of "determination" by the objective requirements of the age, instead of diminishing from the freedom of God, stresses and reasserts it. For, with every change in the nature of the created substance, and the appearance of a new set of problems, and a new type of environment, there should be a new assertion of God's transcending Purpose, and a new application of His creative idea and will, and a new manifestation of His dominating power and values. Such freedom, which is typical of any creative activity, is empirically verifiable, clear and evident, if we take into consideration the life and teachings of the different prophets, and study them in the light of human changing requirements. Such freedom is peculiar to the process of creation, and would not be revealed, if proceeding from God were confined to that of emanation, as Spinoza held it to be. It is through such creative process that God's attributes of perfection, and among them freedom, become manifest, and direct object of human understanding. Hence, it is not quite true to say with Spinoza that "no cause can be given except the perfection of God's nature which extrinsically or intrinsically incites him to action" (Cor. 1). It is also the crying needs of humanity which make God's infinite mercy to pour; and the type of ills that afflict mankind which determine the nature of the remedy prescribed through the teachings of His prophets.

66. PARTICIPATION IN GOD'S CREATIVE PURPOSE IMPARTS RELATIVE FREEDOM TO MAN

Spinoza says, "hence it follows that God alone is a free cause" (Cor. ii). But man was created in the image of God, that is with the capacity to reflect His attributes, which the prophets reveal as "modes" of His nature. If these are creative, man can be as well, if he follows the Purpose which animates them. And to the extent man participates in that creative Purpose, he acquires freedom, and reflects it. For, then he will be free to choose his patterns of behaviour, and free to cast them upon the environment he lives in. And in all such cases he has to take into consideration the nature of the human material found at his disposal, and the type of society he has to recast.

Jesus, for example, set for humanity the example of what constitutes the divine virtues the individual is required to acquire as well as the nature of the Kingdom of God which he has to establish on earth, as the environment wherein that growth can be best effected. He demonstrated the love, perseverance, and self-sacrifice man had to display as well as the meekness and humility he had to practice in attaining that goal. Peter, Paul, and the other faithful followers of Christ were inspired by that vision, and freely chose to dedicate their life to its realization. In other words, they were not constrained to pursue that course; they possessed full liberty to embrace, or to disregard, that Cause. But, by participating in that creative pursuit, they became themselves creative and free: free to give expression to their ideal, free to employ the human material at their disposal, to attain their goal. And the choice, once freely made, steeled their determination. They faced many trials and hardships, but they, and the early Christians after them, finally succeeded in asserting their cultural dominion over the whole Roman Empire. Meekly, but with steady purpose, they finally established the Kingdom, wherein Christian values became supreme. But in all this activity, at every juncture of that long and tragic process, the Christians were faced with an ever new problem and situation which demanded deliberation and positive judgment. Whenever a wave of persecution seemed to engulf them, they were presented the free choice, to recant or endure torture and death. And in the vast majority of cases they freely preferred the latter. There was external compulsion to renounce Christianity, but they chose inner dedication to that noble Cause. The motive power was not a compelling and driving efficient cause but the attraction and love of a formal cause inspiring the early Christians.

When later Islam appeared, to further the spiritual and cultural purpose in the world, a new set of problems were confronted. The vision of the Kingdom of God, or as the Koran termed it, "City of Peace," to be established on earth, remained unchanged, but different circumstances prevailed. Christianity had broken up into warring sects, as a result of doctrinal controversies. Early Islam was presented with totally different human and social material to deal with, a totally new type of "formlessness," than what paganism presented to the early Christians. The need was for a regeneration of man, and a new creation of his social environment. Mohammed had to take into consideration the exigencies of the time, to further God's purposes, and recast the necessary values. The very conception of creation as "improvement," and giving "form" to human nature, and society, implies that the condition of the material to be so improved, or regenerated, must be taken into consideration whether creator be God or man participating in that creative activity. And this creative process involved the operation of a formal Cause, which guided mankind by inspiring it with love, and attracting it with knowledge, and permitting a deliberate free choice.

67. THE DIFFERENCE BETWEEN DIVINE AND HUMAN WILL AND INTELLECT IS BOTH IN NATURE AND MAGNITUDE

In his note to this proposition, Spinoza takes up the question as to whether intellect and will can be attributed to God. The problem is how to avoid anthropomorphism while attributing to God functions peculiar to man, such as intellect and a dominating will and purpose. For God has to be attributed with such perfections, if He is to be considered the source of man's spiritual and cultural life. Spinoza comes to the conclusion that "if intellect and will appertain to the eternal essence of God, something far else must be understood by these two attributes than what is commonly understood by men." In other words, he considers the difference is in the extent and magnitude of the one when compared to the other: that the

132

difference is not of quality but of quantity, though the difference of magnitude is so vast that the same term should be applied only with great reservation. Restricting this difference to magnitude was in full conformity with the ancient Greek idea that generation was through division and addition, rather than formal, that the distinction between the creator and the created was numerical, rather than of quality and kind.

Difference of magnitude, however, does not constitute the sole basis of distinction between divine and human intellect and will. There is also difference in their function and operation, which involves their basic substance. Spinoza admits such qualitative difference, but conceives it as essentially temporal, as priority in time. For he says: "If intellect appertains to divine nature, it cannot, as with our intellect, be posterior (as many would have it) or even simultaneous in nature with the things conceived by the intellect since (Cor. 1, Prop. 16) God is prior in cause alike to all things; but on the other hand, truth and the formal essence of things are such, because they so exist objectively in God's intellect. Wherefore the intellect of God, as far as it can be conceived to form the essence, is in truth the cause of things, both of their essence and their existence. . . . Now as God's intellect is the only cause of things, i.e., the cause of their essence and their existence, it must therefore necessarily differ from them in respect to its essence and in respect to its existence." When Spinoza says, "They so exist objectively in God's intellect," it shows that he understands by generation, as the ancient Greek idealists did, namely, that generation is through division, that there is no essential and qualitative difference between the mind of the creator, and that of the created; just as there is none between a line and the segment divided from it.

68. THE PRIORITY OF THE DIVINE WILL AND INTELLECT IS NOT ONLY TEMPORAL AND CAUSAL, BUT ALSO QUALITATIVE AND SUBSTANTIAL

This priority of the intellect to the essence and existence of things, can be understood in one of two contexts: either in the light of the doctrine of menation, or in that of creation. In either case, the essence of all things, that is, their form and main characteristics, is taken to exist in the divine purpose, or mind, before they are produced, or projected, into the field of nature. The difference is that according to the doctrine of creation the divine purpose, or "Wisdom" revealed by the prophets, is in essence and substance different from human intellect, for the one is creative, and the other passive, unless it participates in God's Primal Purpose. For as we have already stated, human intellect becomes creative only when, and to the extent, it is guided by that purpose. Such being the case, the priority of divine Reason, is qualitatively and substantially, as well as temporally and causally. If on the other hand we consider the question of the priority of divine Reason in the light of the doctrine of emanation, as Spinoza does, we observe that human intellect would then be conceived as a ray of light radiating from the sun, retaining its substance and essence. Because when human intellect is conceived as a mere "outpouring," or radiation, and projection of God's intellect, then the substance and essence of the two would be the same. But revealed religion deems not the doctrine of emanation applicable to human intellect, for it restricts its application to the divine nature revealed in the prophets. This is the basis of the essential unity between divine Reason and the "Wisdom" revealed by the prophets. On this ground Wisdom can say: "I was set up from everlasting, from the beginning of his way before his works of old"(32). That Wisdom being of God is temporally, causally and also substantially and essentially prior to human intellect.

The same principle is stressed by Mohammed in the Koran when he states that only God creates and then imparts to it a new life and being (33). Elsewhere he asks his adversaries whether they can create the world, and then regenerate it, as God does (34). That creative function he considers to be God's alone. The Bab is more explicit when he says in the Bayan that the revealed Word alone creates, sustains, inflicts death, and imparts life (35).

Furthermore, this priority pertains to the Wisdom revealed in all the prophets for we have seen the Koran say categorically that it is heresy, and blasphemous, punishable with eternal fire, to distinguish and divide between the individual prophets, or between these prophets and God Himself. In a similar trend Baha'u'llah says that unity of God implies unity of the prophets, and unity between these and God. Thus, by attributing supreme intellect and will or Purpose to the divine nature revealed in the prophets, as their source, both anthropomorphism and skepticism are avoided. Just as skepticism is overcome only if no separation is made between reality and its appearance, or between different appearances of the same object.

69. NATURE OF THE DIFFERENCE BETWEEN DIVINE AND HUMAN INTELLECT

"A thing that is the cause of the essence and existence of any effect," says Spinoza, "must differ from that effect both in respect to its essence and in respect to its existence. Now the intellect of God is the cause of the essence and existence of our intellect: and therefore God's intellect, in so far as it can be conceived to form part of his essence, differs from our intellect both in respect to its essence and in respect to its existence, nor in any other thing save name can agree with it. . . ." (Note to Prop. 17).

In Prop. 14, Spinoza stated that "except God no substance can be granted or conceived." And in Prop. 15, he said that "whatever is, is in God." How can we reconcile this absolute monism with the statement made here that human intellect and will differ, both in essence and existence, from God's, and that they agree only in name? The answer is that according to Spinoza plurality refers to "modes" and attributes of that substance, not to the substance itself. For though there is unity of substance, there is plurality, or rather infinity, of attributes and modes.

We saw Spinoza establish this monism on the principle of unity of attributes which, he maintains, prevails between God and nature on the ground that they are both infinite; and two infinite substances cannot be admitted as co-existing, and yet, separate. We denied that such a unity of attributes prevails between them, that they are formally alike. For though they are both infinite, their infinity is not of the same nature and hence incompatible. In fact, an infinite creator demands and necessitates an infinite creation; otherwise God's creative power would not be infinite. We contend that God and nature constitute separate substances because, while the one is "unmoved Mover," the other is "moved," while the one imparts attributes of perfection, the other receives and acquires them. Hence such realities with such contrary natures cannot be substantially identified. And the same principle applies to the intellect or "Wisdom" we attribute to them. The essence, nature, and definition of that intellect differs, when applied to the prophets on the one hand, and to man on the other, and therefore cannot be considered qualitatively and formally the same. The one is the "image" of God, as the Bab says, the other merely the mirror which reflects that image.

In this proposition, Spinoza admits that human and divine intellect are different, that the one is active and the other is receptive and passive, but

135

he does not conclude from this that they are substantially different. To him this does not involve contradiction and incompatibility. And the reason for it is the doctrine of emanation to which he subscribed, and which the principle of causal relation does not fully clarify. For causal relation can be either that of emanation or of creation, the one maintains unity of substance, while the other absolutely denies it.

Such predicament lurks in the reasoning of Spinoza because he does not distinguish between the emanation of "Wisdom" peculiar to the divine nature revealed in the prophets, on the one hand, and human intellect on the other. For, according to the doctrine of emanation, difference of essence and existence between God and His "modes" or the divine nature revealed in the prophets does not involve difference of substance. It is otherwise when generation is in the nature of art, or "improvement," that is, creation. The causal relation in the first instant, is in the nature of an overflow, or radiation, of light; in the second it is that of integration, or improvement, effected on an individual reality to produce another and a higher one. In this latter case there is no unity of substance between cause and effect. It is in the light of the doctrine of emanation that Spinoza speaks in his note. Hence, he does not feel that his original monism, and unity of substance, leads him to a basic predicament.

70. THE DISTINCTION BETWEEN ACTIVE AND PASSIVE IN-TELLECT CAN BE VIEWED EITHER IN THE LIGHT OF EMANA-TION OR OF CREATION

Active and passive intellect can be understood, either as the principle of "actuality" and "potentiality," when applied to the sphere of thought, or of "illumination," and "capacity" to reflect that light. That is, it can be understood either in the light of the doctrine of emanation, or of that of creation, of a "hidden" reality manifesting itself within the sphere of human understanding; or of a faculty possessing the capacity to acquire ever new ideas and forms. In the one case substantial unity is maintained between Reason emanating, and Reason emanated; in the other, the source of illumination is substantially different from the mirror which reflects the light.

When "Wisdom" proceeds from God, through the divine nature revealed in the prophets, as a ray of light from the sun, it retains the major premises of thought, as "hidden" potentialities, to be actualized as the occasion arises. When human intellect is said to possess the capacity to reflect the light of understanding revealed by the prophets, then no "hidden" or "innate" ideas and forms are implied to exist in it. In the first case the creative ideas are transmitted as a matter of fact and automatically, as from a principle to his agent; in the second they are taught and diligently acquired: molded into the fabric of human intellect. In the first case the "hidden" potentiality needs mere recollection to be made actual and reveal itself. In the second, the capacity is in possessing the faculty to learn those ideas. The first is peculiar to the divine nature revealed in the prophets; the second is characteristic of human understanding. For God's attributes of perfection are all "innate," "hidden" and "potential" in the prophets. All they need is the occasion to reveal them and the circumstances to practice them as an example for human behavior. In contrast human intellect is a mere capacity, in the sense that man possesses the necessary faculty, which animals and plants lack, to learn and acquire those perfections, with painstaking effort, and adequate guidance.

The active intellect of the prophets, which contains these attributes of perfection as "innate ideas," that is, potentially, and which imparts them, as the occasion arises, to the receptive intellect of man, should be considered as based ontologically upon the principle of unity of substance between God, the Creator, and the divine nature of the prophets, as channel of His revelation. The divine Mind or Intellect is the source and generator of those creative ideas. Hence only that intellect which possesses substantial unity with that of the Creator, and is essentially one with it, possesses those ideas "innately." To every other individual these ideas are forms to be patiently acquired. And because human intellect has merely the capacity to acquire these ideas, or attributes of perfection, it is deemed subject to improvement and evolution.

Thus, in the world of creation, which in the words of the Bab is "other than God," and hence no "hidden" reality exists in it potentially, in it no substantial unity can be deemed to prevail between divine intellect or "Wisdom," and human reason. And as there is no unity of substance between the two, there can be no "innate" ideas in human intellect to reveal themselves as the occasion arises. Man's supreme values, that is, the basic ideas, and forms, which govern his understanding, shape his conduct, guide his development, and mold his rational life, all, are acquired at the feet of the prophets as creators and supreme educators. Human thought has merely the capacity of the wax to receive the imprint of a seal, or of a mirror to reflect the rays of light. As we have observed the Bab say, the "image" is not hidden, or inherent, in the mirror; it is in the reality that emits that light, or in the image itself. In short, potential intellect, which we attribute to the prophets, being based upon substantial unity of their nature with God's, needs merely the occasion to become actual, and reveal itself while human capacity for thought, and understanding, is a mere faculty that can receive that illumination and be guided by it. The first depends on an "indwelling" conception of God, the second on the creative Purpose of an absolutely transcendent One.

71. GOD AS "INDWELLING," AND GOD AS "TRANSCENDENT" CAUSE OF ALL THINGS

Basing his argument on the principle of monism, or unity of substance, held in Prop. 15 and 16, Spinoza now proceeds to interpret causation in that light. "God," he says, "is the indwelling and not the transient cause of all things" (Prop. XVIII). He further states that "God is the cause of all things which are in him," in other words, which are mere emanations of His nature, and segments of His being. This conception is based upon the ancient Greek one which identified the Universe with God, and considered every object in it as a segment, or particle, of its substance and being; and stands in clear contrast to the dictum of the Bab that "all other than God is His creation."

The conception of creation presented in Genesis was interpreted, at the time of Spinoza, as a temporary transient event, which started, and came to a close, within the span of six calendar days. In contrast was the ancient pantheistic conception, also of pagan origin, which viewed God as an indwelling reality, cause, or law, which generated all motion and being. But, granting that the ultimate Cause of all things cannot be a transient reality whose creative purpose started and ended within the period of six days, there is no ground for considering it "indwelling." God, as ultimate and constantly sustaining Cause of all things, can be conceived eternal and everlasting, and also transcendent to nature and to the physical Universe. In fact, this constitutes the conception maintained by revealed religion, and the only one logically tenable.

We have observed that causation can be viewed either in the light of the doctrine of emanation or of creation. An efficient cause can be of the same nature and substance as its effect, or of a totally different one. The trunk is considered the cause of its shoot, a father of his children, and a spring of the river that flows from it. This is the type of causation to which the Bab refers, when he says in the Bayan that God created the Primal Purpose. In other words, the Primal Purpose had the cause of its being in God, inasmuch as it had its source in Him: as a ray of light emanates from the sun. On the other hand, we consider a potter the cause of the formation of a pot, or a sculptor of a statue, or an inventor of his invention. It is in this manner that the Primal Purpose generated all things. Between the members of the first set there is unity of substance and essence; between the latter there is none. In the case of creation proper or generation there is no projection of the substance as a cause but merely the operation of its creative ideas and purpose. We cannot deny causality to the operation of this second type, even though it is not an indwelling, but an absolutely transcendent, cause. For we have observed the Bab definitely state in this connection that "the ocean of divine being cannot enter the sea of created reality; nor the sea of created reality ever pour into the ocean of divine being." In other words, there can be no case of an "indwelling" God, when referring to the world of creation proper.

Furthermore, we have observed that the main interest of revealed religion in the doctrine of creation is in its spiritual and cultural application. And this aspect of human evolution rests squarely upon the formal Cause. For, inasmuch as God, as efficient Cause, reveals Himself as formal Cause, He becomes the creator of man's spiritual and cultural life. And the primary and most essential aspect of a formal cause is that it is formally and qualitatively, and hence essentially and substantially, different from the created reality, which is here the human soul acting as the material cause. The formal, and the material, causes can never be identified without making the very principle of generation nonsense. They can never be substantially the same, when they are essentially and qualitiatively different. The form a sculptor or painter conceives can never be identified with the stone or canvas they use as material to represent the image. The image, the Bab says, is not in the mirror, but in the object reflected, and that implies absolute transcendence of the first to the latter, not "indwellingness."

Thus causation applies to both the actualization of a certain potentiality and also imparting form to a reality acting as material cause, which possesses the capacity to receive that form. We speak of "potentiality" when the effect is an emanation of the cause, and unity of substance and essence is maintained. In such a case no field, no ground, for the operation of a "capacity," to acquire forms originally lacking, remains. In other words, a potentiality which is based upon the principle of an "indwelling" cause, that is, upon unity of substance, is essentially "inherent," not "acquired," even if the occasion has not presented itself to reveal its existence. This is the type of causation which prevails between God and the divine nature revealed in the prophets; but it is inapplicable to the human soul, which is part of the world of creation.

Just as there is no need for acquiring perfection, no scope for growth and "improvement," when the cause is "indwelling," so there is no possibility for relapse, no chance for disintegration and degeneration for the individual or for human society. To put it in the terminology of the Bab: just as there would be no creation and sustained growth, there would be no death, and a new life, and rebirth. And both phenomena, cultural growth and spiritual relapse, are striking recurring events in human history, not to be overlooked. Judaism, Zoroastrianism, Christianity and Islam, in fact all revealed religions, as well as the culture they respectively sponsored and in turn served would have offered no occasion for toil, no field for gradual spiritual growth, and ascendancy; they would not have been followed invariably by decline and recession, if the cause of that spiritual and cultural life were "indwelling" in them and in the institutions they founded. The transcendence of that formal Cause, and the consequent freedom left to man, to accept guidance, rendered both that progress, and that relapse, possible. In other words, "indwelling-ness" of the cause would deprive mankind, individually and socially, of the necessary scope for evolution, reintegration and growth, and will render it changeless. And this is a characteristic of God, and the divine nature revealed in the prophets, not of the world of creation, not of the human soul, and of physical nature.

72. THE ETERNITY OF GOD AND OF HIS ATTRIBUTES

"God," says Spinoza, "and all the attributes of God are eternal" (Prop. 19). To prove this proposition, Spinoza maintains that as God is a substance that necessarily exists (Prop. 7), and His existence follows from His very definition, He is eternal (Def. 8). In other words, God is eternal because He is the unmoved Mover, because His existence does not depend upon the operation of an other than Himself. Furthermore,

Spinoza says that the attributes of God are eternal insofar as they express His essence; for the essence of a thing is co-eternal with its substance. Hence, all His attributes involve eternity.

If we bear in mind that Spinoza identified God with nature, and that by attributes of God he meant "thought" and "body," then we will appreciate the significance of the conclusion that, "each of the attributes must involve eternity." He reached his minor premise and established his conclusion on the ground that nature with its two attributes of thought and extension is an emanation of the divine substance. In contrast to this major premise we have that of revealed religion, namely, that emanation is restricted to the divine nature revealed in the prophets, and that all other things, including thought and extension, are creations of God, and not emanations of His substance.

As we have already observed, the doctrine of emanation is a principle of devolution, of radiation and overflow, not of evolution, integration, and improvement, to a higher state of being. Emanation of the divine Essence is an act of grace, effected to move man who depends upon it for guidance and illumination. But in that act the divine Essence moves, but does not itself move, in the sense of acquiring a higher form of being. And it cannot acquire a higher form of being, because it is initially perfect. It stimulates the motion or evolution of the spiritual life of man, but is not itself subject to such a growth.

Should we consider the world of nature as well, in the light of the doctrine of emanation, as Spinoza does, we would have to deny the possibility of its evolution, progressive integration, and improvement to an ever higher state of being. In that case eternity would imply unchangingness. It would lose its characteristic of everlastingly "becoming," of a never-ending "improvement," a constant motion and promotion. Being initially of divine substance, and hence essentially perfect, it would persist as such. In other words, there would be no metaphysical ground for motion, either in physical nature or of the spiritual and cultural life of man. And the empirical experiences of man cannot endorse such a principle.

If, on the other hand, we restrict the principle of emanation to the divine nature revealed in the prophets, then eternity in the sense of unchangingness becomes the ground of divine guidance, the source of perfect forms man has to acquire in his process of development. It would be an unchanging "Image" of the divine Essence, which man has to set for himself as supreme "example." In contrast, eternity would not imply the unchangingness of the intellectual and spiritual life of man, but an unending scope for progress and evolution. The substance, and attributes, of the divine nature revealed in the prophets, would be the unchanging example, and source of illumination and guidance, and the substance and nature of man, the eternal receptor of that light. And the principle involved is vindicated by historical facts. The divine nature revealed in Moses, Zoroaster, Jesus and Mohammed, as successive emanations, and the eternal and unchanging "Image" of God, became the formal cause of the spiritual and cultural life of man, namely, his thought, moral life, social institutions and aesthetic values, and thereby remolded his being.

73. IN GOD EXISTENCE AND ESSENCE ARE THE SAME

In the previous proposition Spinoza maintained that God and His attributes are eternal. In this one he states that "God's existence and his essence are one and the same" (Prop. 20). In other words, he amplifies the previous principle by considering the divine attributes as mere expressions of the divine Essence; hence its elements are those of His existence, and the two are one and the same. Therefore, as God's attributes are eternal, both His Essence and substance must needs be eternal. As we have, however, shown in our previous discussions, this eternity implies the unchanging nature of both God and His emanations. And this conforms with Spinoza's view expressed in his corollary to this proposition which says: "God and his attributes are immutable."

The divine nature revealed in the prophets, being an emanation of God's substance, and hence of His essence and attributes, is in a state of perfection, and full actuality. It is not a "capacity" to demand motion in the sense of acquiring improvement. Hence it is "immutable." And being in a state of absolute perfection, it can act as adequate source of guidance and illumination to man. It can set the supreme "example" for human activity, the ideal forms man has to acquire in his spiritual and cultural growth. But, if that "immutability" be extended, as Spinoza does, to the reality of man, both physical and intellectual, on the ground that these also are emanations of God's substance, then logically his essence and attributes also will have to be considered "immutable." And that would provide a metaphysical ground for denying even the possibility of regeneration and "improvement" of his cultural life. In such a case the need for a social environment, affording a spiritual and cultural atmosphere for man, would cease to possess any logical necessity. Human nature must be considered as formless matter, subject to the operation of a creative purpose, as clay, with the capacity of assuming an ever higher form, to demand an adequate atmosphere, wherein it can acquire those perfections. Culture implies nurture and capacity for growth and evolution, it does not necessitate immutability of substance and essence on the part of the material used. Were man considered an emanation of God, and the immutability of his nature premised, the possibility of cultural growth will be denied him. For an immutable reality needs no nurture to reveal its hidden attributes of perfection. It can neither acquire higher attributes, nor need it strive towards that end. In short, just as the immutability of the divine nature revealed in the prophets, affords an adequate source for cultural forms, so the capacity of the human soul to acquire ever newer and higher attributes of perfection presents the field and scope for that creative process to operate and bear fruit. These two are complementary: absolutely necessary in the contribution they make for the spiritual life of man.

74. IMMUTABILITY OF ATTRIBUTES APPLIES TO EMANATIONS NOT CREATIONS OF GOD

"All things," says Spinoza, "which follow from the absolute nature of any attribute of God must exist forever and infinitely, or must exist eternally and infinitely through the same attribute" (Prop. 21). This proposition, like many previous ones, can be considered in the light of the doctrine of emanation, and restricted in its scope to the divine nature revealed in the prophets; and thus vindicate itself logically and empirically, or be extended to comprise the world of nature, and the physical and intellectual life of man as well, and thus disclose its inherent flaws, and lead to baffling predicaments, in this field of culture.

Under the doctrine of emanation, any element or particle of the primordial substantial reality is unchanging and eternal, for it is unmoved, uncreated, and in full perfection and actuality. Any change that may seem to overcome it is bound to be modal and accidental to its being. And these modes and accidents are bound to be shed, once it reverts to its initial form. It is otherwise with a creative being, whose

143

individuality is substantial and not modal. With every act of creation, this individual substantial being is reborn, regenerated and assumes a new life and being. It acquires a new form, and is thereby improved, for its individuality and personality become more enriched and marked. Its original stuff recedes into insignificance, when compared to the forms it progressively assumes. What remains abiding and immutable is the will and purpose which created it, sustains it, and imparts to it the new life, as well as the characteristics it thereby acquires. That creative purpose and the forms it assumes are eternal and abiding. All else is subject to change.

Therefore, the basic flaw in the reasoning of Spinoza is that he made the doctrine of emanation apply to the world of nature, including the physical and intellectual life of man, instead of reserving its operation to the divine nature revealed in the prophets. ''Other than God is His creation,'' says the Bab; therefore, they are all moved and regenerated. And the world of creation includes the physical and the intellectual life of man.

Furthermore, it is a flagrant denial of empirical facts to state that nature, or the physical and intellectual life of man, ''must of necessity exist, and that immutably'' (Proof of Prop. 21). Every aspect of human body and thought is changed in its process of growth. Even the individuality and personality of man is made more rich, clear and distinct, in its attributes and perfections, with the process of evolution, and constant regeneration, he undergoes. There is no physical or intellectual element in the child that remains immutable. The same is true if we compare primitive man with the spiritually and culturally evolved. The only immutable element is the creative will and purpose which guide human activity, and the spiritual and cultural forms, the eternal treasures which, as Jesus said, neither moth nor rust does corrupt.

75. THE IMMUTABILITY OF THE IDEA OF GOD

To prove that thought as a mode, or attribute, of God is immutable, Spinoza takes up the idea or conception of the supreme Being, which he considers innate in the human soul, as an example. Thought, Spinoza says, can be limited only by thought. But this idea of God cannot be limited without impairing its nature. Hence, he concludes, it is infinite, eternal and unchanging. ''The idea of God,'' he says, ''necessarily follows from the given thought. Therefore the idea of God in thought . . . cannot have a fixed duration, but through the attribute itself is eternal'' (Proof of Prop. 21).

First, we have to bear in mind that anything in thought is definable, and the idea of God entertained by any branch of philosophy should be definable, otherwise it would not be an object of knowledge and understanding, and therefore, of thought. And being defined, it is limited. It is true that the conception, or definition, will not have ''duration''; but that is in virtue of the fact that it constitutes a universal, and, as subject, not an object to the progression of time. But the lack of a fixed duration does not mean that it had no beginning as a conceived idea, or that it will not cease to be, as such. In fact, the idea of God has a limited reality, by virtue of being definable; and it is on that ground that all revealed religions consider Him unknowable and inconceivable, that it absolutely transcends thought and its definitions. Man can never possess a true idea of God, much less define it.

Furthermore, any idea of God that a school of thought may formulate cannot be considered ''immutable.'' It can always be replacable and modifiable. According to the Bab all things other than God are part of His creation. Hence human thought like human body is part of creation and subject to it. And an idea of God is an element of thought. It can be brought into being and also destroyed. Human thought has a capacity to acquire knowledge, and truth, revealed by the prophets. The idea of God as an eternal truth, is innate, not in human thought, but in the Wisdom revealed by the prophets and imparted to man. In fact, historically, the true conception of God as an absolutely transcendent reality, utterly unknowable and undefinable, with Wisdom as one of His revelations, was imparted by Moses, to replace the conception the Israelites had carried with them out of Egypt. These had a pagan conception which Moses combatted and tried to destroy. The same struggle reappeared between Zoroaster and Jesus, on the one hand, and the heathenism which they confronted, on the other. It was the task of these prophets to eradicate the naturalistic conceptions of God man entertained, and establish in their stead their own, as basis of the spiritual and cultural life they advocated. In short, the idea of God, as part of human thought, like any other conception, is created or generated, sustained and improved, discarded and destroyed, or given a higher measure of objective validity and truth. And in all this evolutionary process it depends upon the guidance afforded by the prophets as the revealers of divine Wisdom.

76. MODIFICATIONS OF ATTRIBUTES OF GOD ALSO EXIST NECESSARILY AND INFINITELY

"Whatever follows from an attribute of God," says Spinoza, "in so far as it is modified by such a modification as exists of necessity and infinitely through the same, must also exist of necessity and infinitely" (Prop. 22). But nothing follows from the nature of God infinitely, and necessarily, except His emanations. Spinoza says here that infinite and necessary modifications of God are also necessary and infinite. In other words, necessary and infinite modifications of God, like the attributes themselves, are immutable. In the following proposition Spinoza says: "Every mode which of necessity and infinitely exists must of necessity have followed either from the absolute nature of some attribute of God, or from some attribute modified by a modification which exists of necessity and infinitely" (Prop. 23).

Spinoza defines "mode" as that which is conceived through another: a "something else"; and hence is distinguished from "substance," which is conceived only through itself. In that sense, a mode of God can be conceived and appreciated only through God, Who constitutes its substance. Such a definition fully applies to the divine nature revealed in the prophets as modes of God, fulfilling His purpose in the world in specific dispensations. For only as revealing His attributes of perfection do they acquire their significance. Only as such can they act as the efficient and formal cause of man's spiritual and cultural life. Being emanations of the divine Substance, and their higher nature "modes" of God's being, their purpose is divine, and the attributes of perfection they reveal are attributes of God, infinite, necessary and immutable. But if we identify nature with God, as Spinoza does, and consider physical "body" and "thought" as its necessary attributes, then necessary modifications of these should also be considered necessary, infinite and immutable. But do facts of history, and of human thought, vindicate the validity of such a major premise? The supreme fruit of nature, and of the physical and intellectual life of man, is the rebirth, and gradual growth, of culture. To follow Spinoza's reasoning and definitions, this would constitute a "mode" of "thought," as an attribute of God, flowing from His

146

substance infinitely, necessarily and immutably. Is that conclusion true to fact? Does the spiritual and cultural life of man reveal that "immutability," which Spinoza's reasoning entails?

77. NATURE OF THE CONTINGENCY OF THE WORLD OF CREATION

"The essence of things produced by God," says Spinoza, "does not involve existence" (Prop. 24). Here he distinguishes between the nature of God, Whose essence involves existence, and the nature of things the essence of which does not involve existence, but rather are produced by Him. These are "modes" of the divine substance, dependent upon God not only for their being or "production" but also for their duration or sustenance. These are so dependent because their essence does not involve their existence.

If "existence" should be defined to refer to "reality," as distinguished from "appearance" then the principle involved in this proposition would apply to the divine nature revealed in the prophets; for this cannot be considered as possessing an existence separate from the divine nature itself. But Spinoza means here, not the reality of the prophets, but individual objects in nature, and particular conceptions in "thought," which he considers to be "modes" of God's attributes.

Now, if nature can be identified in substance with God, as Spinoza does, that is, be considered an emanation of His being, then the spiritual and cultural life of man, the supreme fruit of "thought," would be a "mode" of His substance, which flows from Him infinitely, necessarily and immutably: a conclusion which is contrary to fact. But we would not get involved in the predicaments that arise from such a conclusion if we maintain the doctrine of creation, and consider the spiritual and cultural life of man as the handiwork of a divine "artisan," with man given full freedom to participate in its development. In such a case, the spiritual and cultural life of man would be the sum total of the higher values, or the supreme forms mankind individually and socially can acquire. With this faculty of gradually acquiring those forms, and freedom of accepting or disregarding the guidance of understanding, man becomes subject to an evolutionary process which is neither necessary nor immutable, but rather eternally and infinitely progressive. In short, deny the immutability, infinity, and necessity of the divine nature revealed in the prophets, as

147

the formal cause of human progress; or deny the absolute contingency, freedom, and individuality of the object of creation, and no basis for spiritual and cultural development and growth will remain.

The spiritual and cultural life, therefore, demands the capacity of acquiring perfections: the possibility of integration and disintegration; or, as the Bab would put it, of creation, sustenance, death and rebirth, depending upon the guidance of human understanding by the prophets of God; and the free choice of the individual, and of the group, to accept that guidance or to disregard it. In short, the essence of things "produced" by God do "involve Existence," though only of the contingent type common to all created things.

78. CONTINGENCY OF THE ESSENCE OF THINGS

"God is not only the effecting cause of the existence of things," says Spinoza, "but also of their essence" (Prop. 25). In a corollary he adds: "Particular things are nothing else than modifications of attributes of God, or modes by which attributes of God are expressed in a certain and determined manner." Thus, not only the existence of particular objects, but also their essence, or basic characteristics, is determined. And this is effected, not as part of God's creative purpose, but as an emanation of His substance and being, as "modes" of His nature. Applied to the spiritual and cultural life, the principle entails determination, inner compulsion and immutability. The elements of individual understanding, intellectual guidance, and freedom of choice, will thus vanish; and the spiritual and cultural life will cease to depend upon a formal Cause, as an object of knowledge and contemplation, drawing humanity to itself through love.

"A thing," Spinoza says, "which is determined for the performing of anything was so determined necessarily by God, and a thing which is not determined by God cannot determine of itself to do anything" (Prop. 26). In this proposition, Spinoza proceeds further and says that, this causation is necessary. For the particular object, being a "mode," cannot determine itself, both in existence, and in essence. Being a "mode," both its existence and essence are determined by God, from whose substance it initially proceeded; and that in a manner that is necessary, leaving no vestige of freedom to that "mode" to determine the course it likes to take. For, he says, "a thing which is determined by God for the performing of anything cannot render itself undetermined" (Prop. 27). And when God determines the essence of a "mode" of His own substance, that is,

148

the attributes it has to reveal, this particular object cannot free itself from the necessity and compulsion it entails. Just as the rays which proceed from the sun cannot but manifest the characteristics of its light.

Being an emanation of God, the divine nature revealed in the prophets fully conforms to the principles expressed in these propositions. And the cultural significance of that ''necessity'' is that it makes these prophets truly divine, fully empowered to stand as the formal Cause of man's cultural life, fully representative of the divine attributes of perfection. For God is not only the necessary Cause of man's being, but also of his essence, and of the attributes he has to acquire. And these attributes must needs be revealed for man to appreciate. Being an emanation of God, the divine nature needs selfless channels to reveal itself. And, inasmuch as the prophets are such channels, ''God by the necessity of His nature is the effecting cause of the essence and existence'' they reveal. And when ''determined by God,'' to further His spiritual and cultural purpose in the world, they ''cannot render (themselves) undetermined.'' They cannot but say, as Jesus did, in his agony, ''O my Father, if it be possible, let this cup pass from me: nevertheless not as I will, but as thou wilt'' (36).

On the other hand, were the human soul an emanation of God, as Spinoza deemed it to be, the same determinateness would apply to it. Man's thought, his moral and social life, the aesthetic values he entertains, the urge he feels towards perfection, all would be necessary, and determined, almost automatic. There would be a compelling force arising from its very nature, operating as a ''mode'' of the divine substance. In that case, cultural growth would cease to be the result of understanding and free choice. It would be like honey bees produce instinctively, necessarily, unintentionally, almost automatically, with no moral and spiritual value attached to it.

79. HOW IS HUMAN EVOLUTION DETERMINED?

''A thing,'' says Spinoza, ''which is determined by God for the performing of anything cannot render itself undetermined'' (Prop. 27). Emanation, we have observed, is in the nature of an ''outflow,'' or radiation of the divine Essence. It is the emerging of a mode of being from a universal and primordial substance. Creation, on the other hand, is to define a certain form, and shape the material at our disposal accordingly. In the sphere of the spiritual and cultural life, it is setting before man certain supreme forms: intellectual, moral, social or aesthetic, and bid-

149

ding him contemplate them, appreciate their value and significance, and then seek to acquire them, through repeated practice. In this sphere of the spiritual and cultural life, therefore, there is no direct compulsion of an efficient cause, which "moves" without necessitating freedom of choice and understanding on the part of the "moved," but rather, it starts with knowledge and understanding of the form by the "moved," and then its free choice and conscious pursuit as the means to an ultimate goal.

Now, the setting of that form, as a supreme example for human behavior, is determined by God; for the cyclic course of prophetic dispensations is traced and defined by Him. But the mere fact that He reveals His essence and attributes in the divine nature of the prophets, and makes that the object of human thought, understanding, contemplation, and free choice, proves that God leaves for man scope for self-determination. In other words, God merely guides man, and man is given free choice to avail himself of the guidance, or to disregard it. He leads man to salvation, but does not eliminate the element of free choice; otherwise there would be no basis for moral responsibility in the act and evil just as much as virtue would be positive in nature and compelling. While, in fact, all good is from God, and all evil from man himself. God sheds His light like the sun, indiscriminately. It is the individual heart that turns to it and receives illumination, or turns away and remains in darkness.

In the Persian Bayan, the Bab is explicit on the subject, when he differentiates between the "exalted," and their virtue, and the "non-exalted" and their vice. The nature of the first is positive and good; the nature of the second is negative and evil. There can be no call to negation but only to positive "assentment." Guidance can be only to the "exalted" and positive, not to the "non-exalted" and negative. Evil, therefore, can be only a non-existent and a recession; a falling back, not a positive progress (37). Paradise, which is the supreme attainment of man, is acceptance of God and His prophets, when they appear in the world, and humanity attains their divine presence. Hell is denial of those prophets, and refusal to abide by their law and order. The one is rebirth and eternal life; the other is spiritual death. God, the Bab says, leads only to paradise, rebirth, and a higher realm of being. Death, or deprivation, results from refusal to follow that lead. It is not determined by God; it is the fruit of human stubbornness and waywardness. Love, the Bab says, springs from truth; and other than love from non-truth (38).

80. OBJECTS IN NATURE DETERMINE ONE ANOTHER

"Every individual thing," says Spinoza, "or whatever thing that is finite and has a determined existence, cannot exist nor be determined for action unless it is determined for action and existence by another cause which is also finite and has a determined existence" (Prop. 28). Spinoza here distinguishes between the determination which God imposes upon His attributes, that are infinite and eternal, and these in turn upon their modes, and the determination which prevails between individual finite objects, as modes of God's attributes. These, he says, determine one another mutually and in an endless string of causation. This latter type of determination cannot be directly from God, he says, "for anything that follows from the absolute nature of any attribute of God must be infinite and eternal"; and not limited and individual as things are. "It follows then that it must have been determined for existence or action by God or some attribute of his, insofar as it is modified by a modification which is finite and has a determined existence." But even in this latter case, when finite modes determine one another, we cannot say that God is the "remote cause of individual things," unless we attempt to distinguish these individual things from what follows from the absolute nature of God.

In his note to the proposition Spinoza makes two points which he deems outstanding in significance: first, that individual objects are determined in their existence and action by God; secondly, that "God is the proximate cause of those things immediately produced by him absolutely." Together these points establish the principle of monism and divine immanence. For it maintains that God is the direct and proximate "mover" of all things; which in essence and substance are divine, in the sense that they are "modes" of His being.

We have repeatedly referred to the Bab's principle that other than God is His creation; hence individual, finite objects are not "modes" of His being, but His handiwork. Secondly, that God created the Primal Purpose, and this in turn created all things which are individual and finite. Hence God is not the "proximata" mover, immanent in nature. There is the Primal Purpose, which, as principle of law and order, directs all motion. And this principle is best revealed in the mission of the prophets as creators of the spiritual and cultural life of man. The divine nature revealed in these, is a transcendent reality acting as object of contemplation and understanding, drawing all things to itself through love. In other

151

words, in contrast to the principle of divine immanence and monism maintained by Spinoza to explain the mutual determinem which exists in nature, as modes of God, we have the doctrine of absolute divine transcendence held by revealed religion. In fact, the law and order which we observe in nature, and in the spiritual and cultural life of man, is not the result of only the attraction which prevails between individual things, the manner they act and react to one another. All this action and reaction is dominated by a supreme purpose which is God's. And this principle is best exemplified in the cultural trend of history. The rise and fall of the different cultures have not been due to blind forces operating upon them, but rather the outcome of the divine purpose revealed through the cyclic prophetic dispensations. That is true of the Hebrew, Zoroastrian, Christian and Muslim cultures which succeeded one another, as well as of the Greek and Roman, which were a sort of setback and recession to materialism, when the guiding light of the Primal Purpose seemed remote and little effective. If the divine cultures be considered as "life" to man's spiritual and cultural being, a "creation," as the Bab would consider them, these pagan ones would correspond to what he terms "death," and "negation," of the positive, and dynamic action, of the former. In all these, the creative Cause was the transcendent divine nature revealed in the prophets: a "remote cause," as Spinoza would put it, which was "in no wise connected with its effect," that is, not immanent in it.

81. THE ACTIVE AND THE PASSIVE NATURE

"In the nature of things," says Spinoza, "nothing contingent is granted, but all things are determined by the necessity of divine nature for existing and working in a certain way" (Prop. 29). And the reason for this absolute necessity, which characterises all things, is that God, in whom all things have their being, in the sense that they are emanations of His nature, is not a contingent but a necessary being. For, as Spinoza adds in his proof of the proposition, "whatever is, is in God. But God cannot be called a contingent thing for he exists of necessity and not contingently." Similarly, "the modes of divine nature do not follow from it contingently, but of necessity." In other words, attributes, and modes of those attributes, follow from God, not contingently, but of necessity.

Spinoza then proceeds to state that this absolute necessity, which attached to the reality of all finite things, can be further proven by its converse, namely the fact that if they were not so absolutely necessary they would be impossible; for contingence implies that they determine themselves, and that cannot be admitted. "Wherefore all things are determined by the necessity of divine nature, not only for existing, but also for existing and working after a certain manner, and nothing contingent is granted."

82. THE BAB'S PRINCIPLE OF "BADA"

"Bada" means to revoke a decision already taken and start anew—to re-initiate. The Bab considers it as an essential characteristic of God's creative Purpose. It would apply for example to the manner Jehova revoked His covenant with the Hebrews when they relapsed into heathen practices and iniquity. In the Bayan, he says (39), that immediately the fiat is uttered by the prophet, as the revealer of the creative Purpose of God, the reality of the object comes into being. In other words, all things created by God, that is, all individual finite objects, depend upon that fiat for their being and are determined by it necessarily. But, can we attribute absolute necessity to the Primal Purpose in the pursuit of its creative course? Is God's judgment irrevocable? Do they proceed from Him as necessarily, and eternally, as Spinoza believes His attributes and modes follow from His nature?

We have already observed that freedom cannot be attributed to the divine Essence without involving ourselves in anthropomorphism. But we can predicate that attribute of perfection, to the divine nature revealed in the prophets, to the Primal Purpose which animates them all. An expression of that freedom is the principle of "Bada," or right to revoke a decision already taken, to abrogate a covenant, or institutions which had been enforced and initiate new ones. In the Bayan the Bab considers this principle as an outstanding aspect of God's omnipotence (1). In fact, it constitutes one of God's attributes of perfection in the realm of contingency, and a supreme characteristic of the unfoldment of His creative purpose. Man, the Bab says, revokes a past decision out of incompetence; God revokes through His power and might. It is characteristic of His creative Primal Purpose as revealed through His prophets; for when a law and institution of previous dispensation ceases to be salutary and applicable to the prevailing stage of human evolution, He sets them aside or modifies them. It is this right to revoke and renew them, which renders prophetic dispensations progressive, satisfying the changing needs of humanity, as this latter proceeds on its course of gradual spiritual and cultural evolution. Without this principle of revocation religion would remain static, never answer the progressive needs of mankind, nor help the gradual realization of God's creative purpose.

Thus, only under the doctrine of emanation, and its application to the divine nature revealed in the prophets, as mode of His substance, can we say that the outflow is necessary. With the Bab's principle that "other than God is His creation," that necessity is not absolute, for individual finite objects are not modes of God's nature, but rather a product of art, with God as the supreme artisan. And in such a creative process and improvement the principle of revocation should be considered as supreme. For, creation in pursuit of an ultimate purpose necessitates such a revocation of inapplicable and outgrown laws previously held, and hence their essential contingency.

83. ACTIVE AND PASSIVE REALITIES CANNOT BE SUBSTANTIALLY IDENTIFIED

In his note to Proposition 29, Spinoza states what "we must understand by active and passive nature, for I think that from the past propositions we shall be agreed that by nature active we must understand that which is in itself and through itself is conceived, or such attributes of substance as express eternal and infinite essence, that is God, in so far as he is considered as a free cause. But by nature passive I understand all that follows from the necessity of the nature of God, or of any one of his attributes, that is, all the modes of the attributes of God, in so far as they are considered as things which are in God, and which cannot exist or be conceived without God." Spinoza thus identifies God, the divine substance and essence, from which all things proceed, as "the active nature" and the individual, finite, objects which, according to him, emanate from God's substance as "the passive nature." The first is "active," because He projects His substance in all things; the latter is "passive" because it constitutes the element which is projected, which flows out of His nature, and therefore has the source of its being in Him.

In contrast to this conception of Spinoza, which constitutes in substance what ancient pagan thought maintained, we have observed the doctrine of the Bab that all other than God is His creation, that the ocean of divine being, or substance, does not enter the sea of the created world,

154

nor the sea of the created enter the ocean of divine being. In other words, that individual, finite, objects are not "modes" of the divine substance, but products of God's handiwork, acting as the supreme artisan. All other than God must worship Him, the Bab adds, by reflecting His light, as the mirror does the rays of the sun, and thereby fulfill the purpose of its creation. In the case of man that worship is by pursuing the spiritual and cultural life destined for him.

In the field of the spiritual and cultural life, the "active intellect" revealed by God through the instrumentality of His prophets takes the form of imparting the major premises of thought, the supreme virtues, the social laws and order, and the beauty man requires to attain perfection. Hence "passive intellect" is acceptance, and due application, of those higher forms, on which human understanding, moral life, social institutions, and aesthetic values rest. This implies that the one has its being, and source, in the other as its transcendent cause; that the second possesses merely the capacity to acquire what the other can impart as act of grace; that the one is receptive of forms and characteristics which the other possesses as inherent in its essence; and therefore, that they are not qualitatively alike, but formally absolutely different: as different as an artisan is from the product of his art. And if the two are so qualitatively and formally different, how can they be substantially the same, and one be considered the "mode" of the other? In short, if God is "active" He cannot be identified with nature; and if nature is "passive" it cannot be divine in substance and essence.

84. CAN FINITE INTELLECT COMPREHEND THE ATTRIBUTES OF GOD?

Spinoza states that, "intellect, finite or infinite in actuality must comprehend the attributes of God and the modifications of God and nothing else" (Prop. 30). Spinoza tries to establish here the basic principle of rationalism, namely, that all reality is knowable, even the nature and attributes of God. His reasoning is that, if all finite individual objects, among them human intellect, are "modes" of God, and substantially and essentially one with Him, then "that which is contained in the intellect objectively must of necessity be granted in nature," which, according to the previous proposition, is identical with God. "Therefore," he adds, "intellect finite or infinite in actuality must comprehend the attributes and modifications of God and nothing else." Spinoza might be considered to insert the condition "in actuality" to avoid the objection that finite or human individual intellect having ideas merely potentially might not be conscious of the attributes of God unless they are awakened in its memory. Being in nature divine, the finite intellect of the individual would contain them potentially, until such time as the occasion may arise and he is reminded of their actual existence in his thought.

In contrast to this conception of Spinoza we have observed the Bab say that the finite intellect of man is not in substance one with God's, which is revealed through the prophets; that only in the divine nature revealed in the prophets there are "hidden" ideas, hidden words, awaiting the occasion to express themselves. In the human soul, there is no divine substance, to contain such "hidden," innate, ideas inherent in its very nature. It possesses merely the capacity to acquire those ideas if properly presented, and it is adequately trained to appreciate and love them. And among these ideas are the attributes of God, and the properties and functions of finite individual objects in nature. Science is truths we acquire, and not innately possess.

"A true idea," says Spinoza, "must agree with its ideal, that is (as is self-evident), that which is contained in the intellect objectively must of necessity be granted in nature." That is true if active and passive nature, that is, if divine and human intellect, as well as nature, be substantially and essentially identified, and considered qualitatively the same; not if the principle of creation is maintained, and they are regarded different; not if according to the Bab: other than God be His creation. In such a case, human intellect will be a mere creation of God, with the capacity to reflect those divine attributes. These are not "contained" in it "objectively," they are not "hidden" in its nature, just as the rays of the sun are not "hidden" in the glass which constitutes the mirror.

85. THE EMOTIVE MODES OF THOUGHT ARE ALSO NECESSARY IN THEIR FUNCTIONS.

"The intellect," says Spinoza, "in actuality, whether it be finite or infinite, as also will, desire, love, etc., must be referred not to active, but passive nature" (Prop. 31). In his note to this proposition Spinoza says that by intellect is not meant absolute thought, but only "certain mode of thinking," distinguished as, we might say, individual functions, such as understanding, or will, desire, and love. This intellect is merely conceived through "absolute thought," or through some attribute of God, without which it can neither exist nor be conceived. In other words, by "intellect" Spinoza means here not thought as an attribute of God but as a finite "mode" of that attribute, and includes the emotive elements of will, desire and love. "On this account, like the other modes of thinking, the intellect must be referred not to active but passive nature." Thus, in this proposition, Spinoza identifies intellect in actuality with the human as well, in distinction from the divine.

Spinoza then proceeds to the following proposition and says that "will can only be called a necessary cause, not a free one" (Prop. 32). "Will, like intellect," he says in his proof, "is only a certain mode of thinking, and therefore any single volition cannot exist or be determined for performing anything unless it be determined by some other cause, and this one again by another, and so on to infinity." "So in whatever way it be conceived, whether as finite or infinite, it requires a cause by which it is determined for existence or action: and therefore it cannot be said to be a free cause, but only a necessary one": whether it be an attribute of God, or a mode of that attribute, will as "intellect" is determined by God as the supreme reality and substance from which it proceeds.

Taken in the light of what has preceded, this proposition means that, being modes of "thought," which is an emanation of God's substance, love, will, and desire are just as necessary in their function, they are as finite as individual objects, which are modes of "body." But they are as other attribute of God, determined by an infinite string of causation. The logical outcome of this reasoning is brought out in the two following corollaries: first, "hence it follows that God does not act from freedom of will"; secondly, "that will and intellect hold the same place in the nature of God as motion and rest, and that, absolutely, as with all natural things which must be determined by God in a certain way for existence and action."

Just as these conclusions follow logically from the major premise of Spinoza, namely, the emanation of all things from God and their unity of substance with Him, so the conclusion of revealed religion, stands in absolute contrast to it, because of the major premise it accepted, and which was founded on the doctrine formulated by the Bab, namely that "all other than God" is His creation. It is true that the Primal Purpose or will of God, like His "Wisdom," flows out of His nature and substance

157

with the same necessity as the rays which emanate from the sun; but that Primal Purpose transcends human will, love, and desire. It creates them and gives them form. It regenerates this human will, by overcoming its formlessness, and giving it a new direction and individual being. And thus formed by the Primal Purpose, this will, love and desire become objective and real. Otherwise they remain as inchoate "matter" with mere capacity to be formed, guided, and galvanized.

Being part of the physical universe, every atom of being is bound to every other, according to specific, necessary laws of causation. In animate life, this mutual attraction and law and order is directed towards a certain goal, namely the birth and sustenance of the organic whole as an individual, finite being. These function on the level of nature, and are determined by it, through a string of causation which is infinite. This mutual attraction, and binding force, may be figuratively termed will, desire and love as Plato did in his symposium. But when we ascend the scale of being to man, and proceed to consider his spiritual and cultural life, that will, desire, and love obtain a new and different significance. They become a field of activity in which man can, and must consciously participate, to reveal his creativeness and evolve. And participating in that creative activity, he acquires the freedom which is characteristic of the creator. The instincts of animals might be figuratively termed will, desire and love, but these obtain a totally new significance when applied to the spiritual and cultural life of man. For, the guidance which the prophets of God impart to the human soul is not a necessary cause, but an intelligent and free one. It cannot be compared to fire, which as an efficient cause burns, but to light and illumination, which guide, attract, and lead on to our destiny. As formal cause of human evolution these prophets reveal the beauty of God's attributes, and make them positive objects of thought, understanding and contemplation, as well as of attraction, will, desire and love, which the individual is free to accept, follow, and be saved by, or to disregard, deny, and die. Peter and Paul were not driven by blind instincts which shaped their will, desire and love for Jesus, and his promised kingdom of God. They freely and willingly accepted that call. In short, just as the "active intellect," as "Wisdom," does not act automatically, and necessarily, in the "passive intellect" of man, so the "active will," as Primal Purpose, revealed by the prophets, is not a compelling, necessary, efficient cause, but rather, it operates as a formal cause which stimulates the will, awakens desire, and stirs love in the human heart, leaving full scope for intelligent and free choice to the individual, in the realization of his spiritual and cultural destiny.

86. IS THE NATURE OF THE ORDER OF THE UNIVERSE NECESSARY?

"Things," says Spinoza, "could not have been produced by God in any other manner or order than that in which they were produced" (Prop. 33). A proof for this proposition is that all things emanate from God's substance, and hence are determined in nature and motion by it. "If things could have been of another nature or determined in another manner for action so that the order of nature were different, the nature of God could be different than it is now."

We have observed that in the field of the spiritual and cultural life which is the field of religion proper, individual human beings are born merely with the capacity of acquiring perfection, and hence actually bereft of them, that only after adequate knowledge and understanding of those perfections, and their free choice as principles of thought and conduct, can man evolve and progress on the road to perfection. In other words, human thought and free will are determining factors within certain limits of operation. And the reason for it is that God does not act in this realm as "efficient Cause" alone but also as formal cause of that development. And a formal cause demands not blind, automatic, and necessary response to its call; but rather, intelligent and free mode of choice and behavior on the part of man. That initial lack of perfection and the subsequent possibility of inadequate understanding of what constitutes virtue and what the wrong choice and mode of behavior present the prophets as revelations of God's Primal Purpose an ever new material to remold, and recast, in pursuit of their end. The reasoning of Spinoza would have been applicable, if the human soul were an emanation of God's substance, and hence initially perfect, and also if its behavior were determined solely and absolutely by God as efficient cause. In that case individual understanding and freedom of choice would not possess a field to operate, as determining factors of spiritual and cultural evolution. In other words, under the doctrine of creation, there can be "order" as well as "disorder" in human society, "form" as well as "formlessness," "life" as well as "death," with all the variety of grades between these two extremes; all depending on the extent to which man merges his will in that of God's Primal Purpose as revealed by the prophets.

87. THE PRINCIPLE OF CONTINGENCY

In the first note appended to this proposition, Spinoza tries to show "that there is absolutely nothing in things by which we can call them contingent." To explain the nature of contingency, he starts by defining the terms "necessary" and "impossible." The necessary, he says, is "either by reason of its essence or its cause. For the existence of anything necessarily follows either from its very essence or definition, or from a given effecting cause. A thing is said to be impossible by reason of these same causes." In other words, the essence and nature of the efficient cause, what is here termed the "given effective cause," determines either the necessity, or the impossibility of the effect, in its existence and action, based on whether there is compatibility and harmony, or contradiction, between the two. If, therefore, anything is considered "contingent" or "possible" it is, according to Spinoza, only because of the imperfection of our knowledge of the "effecting cause," not because of any lack of determinism on its part. "For when we are not aware that the essence of a thing involves a contradiction, or when we are quite certain that it does not involve a contradiction, and yet can affirm nothing with certainty concerning its existence, as the order of causes has escaped us, such a thing can seem neither necessary nor impossible to us: and therefore we call it either contingent or possible."

We have, however, observed that in the field of the spiritual and cultural life the ultimate cause is not merely "effective" but also formal: not only "compelling" through a universal law of prophetic cycles, and a dominating Primal Purpose, but also "guiding" human reason, and leaving ample field for freedom of choice to the individual, either to participate in that creative process and "live," or remain unmoved and "die." And this operation of human understanding and freedom of choice are not only the elements which impart moral responsibility, value and significance to conduct; but they are too obvious to be denied.

In his second note to Prop. 33, Spinoza says "that things were

160

produced by the consummate perfection of God, since they followed necessarily from a given most perfect nature.'' The perfection of God's nature is beyond questioning but the point of divergence centers around the meaning we attribute to the term ''produced,'' in the above quotation: whether it is in the nature of emanation, that is, projection of the divine substance, or generation of a new reality, as an object of art. For in the first case, the determining force is solely the nature of the substance projecting itself; while in the latter the material at the disposal of the artisan presents its own conditions, which he has to take into consideration, to pursue his creative purpose accordingly.

If individual, finite, human souls, or the law and order dominating society, were emanations of God, or ''modes'' of His substance, that is, if they were in essence divine, there would be no possibility of spiritual and cultural recession, no fall to the level of materialism and naturalism, no ''death,'' as the Bab would term it. The efficient cause cannot be immanent in a certain reality, and yet be inoperative. In the second corollary of Prop. 32, Spinoza speaks of infinite things following from ''motion and rest''; there can be no ''rest'' if the cause is ''efficient,'' and immanent in objects of nature. The fact of spiritual and cultural ''rest,'' ''death,'' or recession can be explained only through the existence of a formal cause, which transcends those objects, and acts as possible source of guidance to human thought and will. In other words, contingency arises, not from any imperfection in the divine nature, but from the immature understanding, and wrong choice, of the individual when confronting the privilege of participating in God's creative purpose. In short, the existence of ''possibility'' or ''contingency'' in the spiritual and cultural life is not due to imperfection in God's nature but to the field of freedom of choice permitted to man.

Thus, the contingency of man's spiritual and cultural condition, as well as of the social order under which he lives, is not because God does not will, and the Primal Purpose does not pursue, those ends; it is because in God's plan these are to be perfected intelligently and freely on the part of man. For only thus can they rise beyond the sphere of nature, where things are compelled to be, by an efficient cause, to a level where they are intelligently pursued and freely sought. Participation of human understanding and freedom of choice renders the spiritual and cultural life of man essentially contingent. It is the fact that he possesses merely the "capacity" of acquiring perfection that renders his condition contingent and makes the principle of "possibility" prevail.

88. NATURE OF THE POWER OF GOD

In the last three propositions of his chapter concerning God, Spinoza tries to show that "the power of God is the same as his essence" (Prop. 34); that "whatever we conceive to be in the power of God necessarily exists" (Prop. 35); and that "nothing exists from whose nature some effect does not follow" (Prop. 36). All these three conclusions, presented in the form of propositions, are logical conclusions from his premises, based upon the doctrine that all things emanate from the substance of God, or are modes of His nature.

Power, or what has been termed Sovereignty, Kingdom, and Dominion in religious literature, like any of the other attributes of perfection, when predicated of God, leads to anthropomorphism, and to the formulation of a conception of God along lines man regards as essentially human in virtue and perfection. It is only when predicated of the divine nature revealed in the prophets that these attributes acquire an objective significance, and become truly divine; for only then do they express in thought, words and deeds, a positive form, or example, for mankind to follow and acquire in the process of its spiritual and cultural evolution.

That power can be observed in the law and order the prophets have actually established in the life of the individual as well as of the society in which he is destined to live. Now, is this Power, this spiritual and cultural Sovereignty and Empire the prophets established, and of which history presents ample facts, the result of a "necessity," or is it the fruit of a "guidance," involving an intelligent, and free, choice on the part of man? Is it realized through "compulsion," the driving force of an efficient cause; or the attraction and love of a formal cause which stands as an object of contemplation and beauty?

Jesus said, "Be ye therefore perfect, even as your Father which is in heaven is perfect"(40), and also "I have given you an example, that ye should do as I have done to you"(41). In other words, he bid mankind seek perfection; and consider his own words and deeds as supreme examples of those divine virtues. By setting the supreme example, he sought to establish his empire over the spiritual and cultural life of mankind. Therefore, his dominion and sovereignty was not the type that drove men to individual perfection as their goal; but rather of the kind that called man to higher, and nobler, forms and states of being. That spiritual and cultural dominion was not the result of compulsion, but the fruit of understanding, free choice and love. Similarly, when we read his parables regarding the Kingdom of God to be established on earth, we see him try to present a picture of the ideal state of human society, as a social "form" which demands understanding, permits free choice, and awakens desire and dedication; rather than as a force, an efficient cause that drives mankind to a prescribed destiny.

NOTES

(1) Prayers and Meditations of Baha'u'llah, tr. by Shoghi Effendi CXIV.

(2) The Persian Bayan, by The Bab 4:1

(3) The Persian Bayan, by The Bab 4:6.

(4) Gleanings from the Writings of Baha'u'llah, tr. Shoghi Effendi LXXXIII.

(5) Ibid. I.

(6) The Persian Bayan, by the Bab 4:6

(7) Ibid. 4:1.

(8) The Persian Bayan, by the Bab, 4:10.

(9) Ibid. 4:1.

(10) The Persian Bayan, by The Bab 4:6.

(11) The Persian Bayan, by The Bab 4:6.

(12) Gleanings from the Writings of Baha'u'llah tr. by Shoghi Effendi XIX.

(13) Gleanings from the Writings of Baha'u'llah, tr. by Shoghi Effendi XXVII.

(14) Matthew 10:34.

(15) 1 Cor. 15:44.

(16) Gleanings from the Writings of Baha'u'llah, tr. by Shoghi Effendi XXVI.

(17) The Persian Bayan by The Bab 4:1.

(18) Ibid. 4:6.

(19) The Persian Bayan, by The Bab, 4:1.

(20) The Koran 4:150.

(21) Gleanings from the Writings of Baha'u'llah, tr. by Shoghi Effendi XXII.

(22) Gleanings from the Writings of Baha'u'llah, tr. by Shoghi Effendi CLX.

(23) Gleanings from the Writings of Baha'u'llah tr. by Shoghi Effendi CLIII.

(24) Matthew 7:20.

(25) The Koran 67:2.

(26) Gleanings from the Writings of Baha'u'llah, tr. by Shoghi Effendi XCIII.

(27) John 8:23.

(28) The Persian Bayan, by The Bab 7:7.

(29) Gleanings from the Writings of Baha'u'llah, tr. by Shoghi Effendi LXXVIII.

(30) Gleanings from the Writings of Baha'u'llah, tr. by Shoghi Effendi, LXXXII.

(31) Gleanings from the Writings of Baha'u'llah, tr. by Shoghi Effendi, XXVII.

(32) Proverbs 8:23.

(33) Koran 30:27.

(34) Koran 10:34.

(35) The Persian Bayan 4:8.

(36) Matthew 26:39.

(37) The Persian Bayan, by the Bab, 9:7.

(38) Ibid. 9:8.

(39) The Persian Bayan, by the Bab 2:1.

(40) Matthew 5:48.

(41) John 13:15.

APPENDIX

1. THE FOUR CAUSES OF HUMAN EVOLUTION

As early as Aristotle we find the distinction made between the efficient, the formal, the final and the material causes. Where the distinction first originated we cannot tell, though they are defined and distinguished best in revealed religion. The tendency of Aristotle himself was to set aside their logical and metaphysical differences, and merge them into one single existent reality, to satisfy his monistic inclinations. In his physics he identified the efficient with the formal cause, to constitute the "unmoved mover," and in his metaphysics made forms immanent in physical nature, thus joining the two in actual existence. With his belief, that the human soul is merely the form of the body, and hence destroyed with it, he could not make it the object of the final cause, retaining perfections it acquires in higher realms of being. He thus tended to make the final cause of human evolution, together with the efficient, formal and material causes, all imminent in physical being.

But in identifying the formal with the efficient cause, Aristotle advocated a dynamism, the outcome of which is to consider the material consciously seeking the higher forms. In his system the seed, for example, possesses an inner urge to become a tree, and the embryo full maturity. Descartes found that principle inapplicable to physical being. No urge, for example, could be attributed to a stone to fall, or move in a specific direction. It was moved, he saw, by forces in direct contact with it, and exerting influence from outside. Hence, the cause was solely efficient, not formal as well. We have observed that, though this principle may be true of physical being, that an efficient cause can fully explain all phenomena of physical nature, the existence of a formal cause is of paramount necessity for the spiritual and cultural life. For only by contemplation, understanding, and desire of that transcendent form can man acquire perfection, and proceed in his process of evolution. And that formal cause, and unmoved mover, we identified with the divine nature revealed in the prophets. We found that the existence of that formal cause renders man's spiritual and cultural life and growth intelligent and free, rather than constrained and automatic as the phenomena of nature are. That elimination of the formal cause, as a transcendent reality, centered in the divine nature of the prophets, constituted the basic flaw in the system of Descartes, as well as of Spinoza.

2. THE PRINCIPLE OF FINAL CAUSE AND THE DOCTRINE OF CREATION

But Spinoza's monism, like Aristotle's, could not countenance the existence of a separate and distinct final cause of human evolution. It would have been disturbing to his conception of the human soul as in substance divine. So he tries to refute its existence in the Appendix to his chapter concerning God. We saw, in dealing with his propositions concerning God, that these are all logical deductions from his major premise that all things, whether in the nature of "thought," or "body," or "modes" these may assume to constitute individual finite objects, are mere emanations of God: that they are in substance and essence one in nature with Him. In contrast we observed the dictum of the Bab, that all things, other than God, are His creations, mere mirrors reflecting His light. This, he maintained, was the major premise of the system of thought advocated by revealed religion. Now, in dealing with the existence of a final cause, of human evolution, its nature and goal, we find the same two basic doctrines of emanation and creation presenting contrasting and rival attitudes and significance. The one tends to deny the existence, and efficacy, of a distinct final cause, the other lays stress upon its reality and eternal operation.

3. THE ATTITUDE OF SPINOZA

He says: "Now since all these misunderstandings which I am undertaking to point out depend upon this one point, that men commonly suppose that all natural things act like themselves with an end in view, and since they assert with assurances that God directs all things to a certain end (for they say that God made all things for man, and man that he might worship God), I shall therefore consider this one thing first, inquiring in the first place why so many fall into this error, and why all are by nature so prone to embrace it; then I shall show its falsity, and finally, how these misunderstandings have arisen concerning good and evil, virtue and sin, praise and blame, order and confusion, beauty and ugliness, and other things of this kind." Spinoza says that man is prone to attribute to natural phenomena a final cause, because "all men are born ignorant of the causes of things, and that all have a desire of acquiring what is useful; that they are conscious, moreover, of this. From these premises it follows then in the first place that men think themselves free inasmuch as they are conscious of their volitions and desires, and as they are ignorant of the causes by which they are led to wish and desire, they do not even dream of their existence. It follows, in the second place, that men do all things with an end in view, that is, they seek what is useful. Whence it comes to pass that they always seek out only the final causes of things performed."

Spinoza thus considers the belief in the existence of a final cause to be devoid of objective validity, to be essentially subjective to man, and due to a "necessary estimation" of other natures by their own. "And as they know that they found these things as they were, and did not make them themselves, herein they have cause for believing that someone else prepared these things for their use." And this someone else is deemed to be God. "This was the reason why all diligently endeavored to understand and explain the final causes of all things." This belief in a final cause permeating natural phenomena, Spinoza proceeds to say, is the ground for many of the superstitions that dominate the mind of the masses, when they ascribe a good or evil intention to them. It is all the result of lack of understanding of the efficient causes which dominate them in fact. The only remedy he prescribes for eliminating this ignorance is the study of "mathematics, which deals not in the final causes, but the essence and properties of things" which operate as efficient causes.

4. THE SIGNIFICANCE OF THE FINAL CAUSE IS FULLY REVEALED IN THE HISTORY OF THE SPIRITUAL AND CULTURAL LIFE OF MAN

"Nature," says Spinoza, "has no fixed aim in view"; "things in nature proceed eternally from a certain necessity and with the utmost perfection." These statements are true and can be confidently asserted, if applied to physical being. To make the final cause imminent in nature entails the same results as to make the formal cause imminent in it. Seemingly, "nature has no fixed aim in view," just as it has no conscious urge for a specific form. To have a fixed aim implies reason and consciousness; and these faculties cannot be attributed to an unintelligent physical being. They spring into existence only in the spiritual and cultural life of man. Mathematics does not deal with final causes, but solely with the properties of things and their functions, because it applies primarily to physical objects where the efficient cause prevails. In other words, Spinoza errs when he adds that "all final causes are merely fabrications of men," that they are of a subjective nature and origin, that they are "modes" of human imagination, devoid of objective validity and significance.

The fact is that final cause begins to reveal its full significance and value when nature is made material for the creativeness that the spiritual and cultural life entail. In that case even the physical senses of man are subjected to the interpretation of reason and its power to project itself back into the past, and recall its experiences, or project itself into the future with plans and hopes. And these plans and hopes constitute the final causes of man's activities, and his spiritual and cultural life. For physical senses detect temporary fleeting events, while reason can detach itself from the immediate present, view the past, and sketch for the future. And that is the realm of the spiritual and cultural life, where reason prevails. In other words, the final cause, like the formal one cannot be immanent in the material; and that is clear and evident, resting in fact in the spiritual and cultural life of man as its supreme field of expression.

5. GRADATION OF BEING NECESSITATES THE EXISTENCE OF A FINAL CAUSE TO PERMEATE AND UNITE IT

Spinoza rightly maintains that mathematics does not discover a final cause for being; but that is because it reduces all things to homogeneous number. It eliminates gradation of being. In existence, however, there is no such abstraction of being. There is a process of evolution from a lower stage to a higher one. And that process, to be one and continuous, binding organically the different strata of being, requires the operation of a final cause, or dominating purpose. The end is served only when the properties and functions mathematics discovers are used to serve the final cause, or the higher reality. Only then they acquire significance and value. Physical elements, for example, reveal a final cause of their being only in the light of the needs of plant and animal life. The coming into being, sustenance, and increase of this latter, determine the final cause of the former. Similarly the appearance of man defines the final cause of physical elements, as well as plant and animal life, for these provide the habitat and environment wherein the latter is to be born, sustained, die and acquire a nobler existence. This is not a "fabrication of man," but a principle ingrained in a universe which is subject to constant creation and regeneration, and where there is a stratification of being and evolution and "improvement." It is not a belief subjective to man, it is a law objective to the universe, as a created and ever evolving reality.

This principle is detected as an objective truth, not only in the appearance of man as an individual, and the highest form of life, in the physical universe, but also in the evolution of the spiritual and cultural life itself. The Bab is definite on that subject in the Persian Bayan. Every subsequent manifestation, he says, is the goal for which the previous one was revealed (1); in other words, it constituted the final cause of the whole series that went before it. The purpose of every prophetic dispensation is to make humanity ready for the adequate reception of the subsequent one, as constituting a higher and fuller revelation of God's creative project for man. And in this field, of the spiritual and cultural life, God is eternally confronted with new circumstances, a new creative task, and a new order of things (2). It is on this ground that every subsequent prophetic dispensation is "the Day of Judgment" of the previous one; "the Paradise," or period of fruition, to which it beacons as a final cause. The revelation of the Primal Purpose, through these successive prophetic dispensations when considered as one, constitutes an evolutionary process, with a gradation of stages through which humanity has to pass. Hence every previous dispensation acquires its specific significance, and value, in the light of the subsequent one; that is, in the measure it furthers human understanding for its reception. This purpose, or final cause, is not as Spinoza conceived it, a figment of human imagination, but rather, the sine qua non of any process of evolution, creation and growth. Therefore, it is the conception of the Day of the Lord, visualized by the prophets of Israel; the final turning point of civilization, as expressed by Zoroaster; the Kingdom of God on earth foretold by Jesus; the inauguration of the City of Peace, mentioned in the Koran; the Unity of Mankind to which Baha'u'llah calls humanity, it is that conception which constitutes the final cause of the intellectual, moral, social and aesthetic evolution of mankind down the ages. It is in the light of this supreme state of man's spiritual and cultural attainment that his previous stages of development can be valued and appreciated. That constitutes the final cause of his culture and civilization.

6. DOES THE EXISTENCE OF A FINAL CAUSE CONTRADICT GOD'S INITIAL PERFECTION?

"I have shown," says Spinoza, "that all things in nature proceed eternally from a certain necessity and with the utmost perfection. I should add, however, this further point, that the doctrine of final causes overthrows nature entirely. For that which in truth is a cause it considers as an effect, and vice versa, and so it makes that which is first by nature to be last, and again, that which is highest and most perfect it renders imperfect." Further he states, "But if those things which are immediately produced by God are made by Him for the attaining of some end, then it necessarily follows that the ultimate things for whose sake these first were made must transcend all others. Hence, this doctrine destroys the perfection of God: for if God seeks an end, He necessarily desires something which He lacks."

Two points are brought out in these two quotations: first, that it makes what by nature comes first to appear the last; secondly, that it entails the existence of imperfections in the divine substance, which God has gradually to discard. Now, the final cause constitutes the goal of what the Bab terms "primal Purpose"; for "Purpose" implies, not only an initial mover, but also the aim which the primal Purpose entertains, that is, the goal of the creative process. If all things, says the Bab, in his introduction to the Persian Bayan, had tasted of God's love, all, because of this love, would have been illumined. This illumination generates light, resides in light, and ends in light. With this light, God guides whomsoever He wishes. It is, for certain, the initial and the final cause. If the initial source of light be identified with the divine nature revealed in the prophets, the final cause would be that same light after being acquired by man. In other words, just as the divine attributes revealed by the prophets constitute the formal cause of human evolution, their ultimate acquisition by man is the supreme end of his "improvement" and evolution. Though initially they spring from the primal Purpose of God, they become the "forms" man acquires.

Should we adopt Spinoza's point of view, and consider all things as emanations of God, and projections of His substance and essence, that is, mere modes of His being, then what should be rightly considered the initial source of perfections would be also the final product. For the initial and the final cause would be substantially identical. But if we adopt the principle of creation as "improvement," maintained by revealed religion, then no unity of substance between the Creator and the created is assumed. The one would be the source of all "forms," in their full actuality and perfection; the other eternally remain reliant on the generating and sustaining power of the first. The first ever absolute in substance and essence; the second ever contingent, both in substance and attribute.

Secondly, does the existence of a final sense imply the existence of initial imperfections in the divine substance, as Spinoza maintains? With the major premises he had adopted, namely, that all things are in substance one with God, differering only as modes and attributes, such conclusion is logical and necessary. For either God's substance is initially perfect, and, therefore, needs no final cause to acquire it, or it is imperfect, and hence not absolute in being. In that case He would be part of the contingent world, and subject to "improvement."

No such predicament, however, is entailed by the principle of creation, as defined by the Bab. For, God, he says, absolutely transcends all things. His substance cannot be considered in anything, or end in anything. All things, like mirrors of different dimensions, capacity and purity, merely reflect His essence and attributes. Such forms as we observe are located in His Primal Purpose as their source, not in the glass of which the mirror is made. The latter has merely the "capacity" to reflect that light or image. Imperfections constitute limitations of the glass, not of the effulgent rays that pour upon it. According to Baha'u'llah and the Bab, the human soul is not in substance one with God, not a particle of His divine stuff and being, not a "mode" of His reality. It is a formless non-physical matter seeking perfections. Man has to seek, attain, contemplate and acquire those infinite perfections, to fulfil the purpose for which he has been created.

NOTES

(1) The Persian Bayan, by the Bab 2:17.
(2) Ibid. 2:15.